HANDLING THE TEENAGE YEARS

A life resource for all young people and adults, who care for them.

Ebenezer Opeyemi Anifowose

Handling the Teenage Years
Copyright © 2019 Ebenezer Anifowose.

ISBN 978-978-952-765-6

Unless otherwise stated, all Scripture are taken from the New Living Translation © 1996, 2004, 2007 by Tyndale House Publishers

Published by:
Ebenny Innovative Consults (Ebenny Inc.)
P.O.Box 125, Sango Ota
Ogun State, Nigeria.
ebennyinc@yahoo.com

CONTENTS

DEDICATION

This book is dedicated to the loving memory of my beloved brother, Emmanuel Olufemi Anifowose. You were my inspiration in every sense of the word. You lived your life like an open book and you blessed the world with every page of it.

ACKNOWLEDGEMENT

I acknowledge everyone who had contributed to this book in one way or the other. Friends who helped edit and review the book, Aanu Bello, Moyo Adesanya, Gbolawa Ogidan, Edward Enejoh, Yinka Soremekun and Funmi Omobowoje. I cannot thank you enough for your significant input. My gratefulness knows no bounds.

I also thank the teenagers that read the manuscript and gave me the initial feedback that has helped in shaping this book further. I appreciate every teenager who allowed me the humble privilege of mentoring them. My many talks with you were learning experiences for me. You indeed helped develop the ideas in this book. I cannot but mention Tosin Duyile and Juwon Ibrahim. Thank you very much.

Baba and Mama Anny, you have given me the freedom to express myself. You support me in all of my pursuit and dreams including the risky ones. Thanks for believing in me. I love you. Thanks to my siblings for bearing with me all the while I buried myself in my computer. You are highly treasured.

PREFACE

This book in your hands is a product of 4 years of inspiration, writing, research, understudy and engaging young people in different settings plus an additional 5 years of testing its ideas in the real world. This year, the book was updated and it is safe to say that there is no better time than now to bless the world with it.

Precisely, five years ago when I initially finished writing this book, I felt a bit of 'did I really write a book?' 'Will readers find it worthwhile?', 'What will people think?' Like most first time authors, I also had that feeling of been unsure. Moreover, I had every reason to feel so because I started writing this book when I was 19 years old. I was just leaving the teenage bracket myself but was so interested in sharing with other young people the help I had received and the understanding I gained while breezing through the unfolding and adventurous years as a teen. This book was written by a teenager and updated as an adult who has gained experience working with young people. It is a book written by a teenager with a first-hand experience of what it feels like to be one.

I am convinced it is a book that will help you as a teenager to understand yourself at this critical stage of life. If you are a parent or guardian, you can read this book to gain some insight into how to relate with teenagers and young people. Of course, you were once a teenager and therefore also have a firsthand experience which I would say is invaluable.Teenagers are encouraged to read this book carefullyand carry their parents or guardians along if possible.

To effectively use this book as a resource, have a notepad with you with which you can take notes and to answer the very important questions you will see as you read. These questions should stir your thoughts and as much as you can, try to provide answers even if it takes you days to put your thoughts together. In addition, there is a 'work to do' section and an 'activity' section at the end of each Teen Focus and a 'bonus activity' section in Teen Focus #4. Take your time to answer them carefully.

The book has also been written in such a way that it can be read as a 'snack'using the section headings. I do hope you enjoy reading this book as much as I enjoyed writing it and it is my prayer that every page of it brings you light and blesses you.

So far, So God.

Ebenezer Anifowose
June 2015

INTRODUCTION

At home,

Uncle Ebbie,

I got your gift inthe post. I liked it, thank you. I expected you would attend my 15th birthday party but mum told me you travelled. Mum made me a large cake and I had lots of fun. How is aunty and my friends, Rose and Frank?

Uncle Ebbie, when are you visiting? I need to talk to you, about a whole lot of things. Sometimes I feel like I am carrying heavy weights on my shoulders. I am under pressure at home and in school. That boy i told you about, he has told me he wants us to be special friends. I think I like him, but I am confused and do not know what to do. What should I tell him? Should I date him?

Uncle, I have issues with my mathematics classes. I am not able to answer the home assignments. The class is always boring and I did not pass my last test.

Dad has been upset about this. He doesn't let me go out with my friends anymore. He tells me he is protecting me but I do not understand what that means. He is not letting me have fun because he is protecting me? Mum complains about my room being untidy every time, she wants me to clean up every day. To me, my room looks clean but mum always disagrees.Can you

Imagine she wants me to dust the room every weekend and I told her, I think twice a month should be just fine. She doesn't seem to think I am entitled to any opinion of mine.

Uncle, I am 15 years old now and Dad tells me I have to go to bed by 10p.m He will not let me watch the TV or use my phone after then. Church on Sundays are always boring, and they will not let me just stay at home.

I love mum and dad so much but sometimes it just feels like they hate me. I know they don't but they don't give me any space. As I see it, my brother is always right but I am always wrong.

I wish you will come to visit soon. You are the only person I can talk to about what bothers me. Do hurry up and come to visit. I know dad will listen to you.

You know I like to read from you. I can't wait to receive your letter in the post. One more thing uncle, can you send me a book to read? I have finished the one you gave me the last time.

Greetings to Aunty, Rose and Frank

It's me,
Teen

TEEN FOCUS #1
YOU & YOURSELF

A wise child brings joy to a father, a foolish child brings grief to a mother – Prov. 10:1

Dear Teen

You have come a long way, thirteen years at the least, to be called a teenager. Now you begin to understand yourself, you begin to know and analyze your emotions and you can now express your feelings better. You begin to identify your strengths- things you are good at, and your weaknesses- things you are not so good at. You sense in yourself that you are growing up and becoming mature. You just want to be different.

The teenage years are full of hopes and anxiety, fears and cares- withal mix of not knowing what to do. You feel good about yourself anyway, that you are also becoming an adult and you feel on top of the world when you are promoted to the next class.

You should know that another name for the teenage years is adolescence and the teenager is referred to as an Adolescent. As a teen, a lot of things are happening to you that you do not even understand yourself(although you think you do) and in your candid opinion, almost everyone around you also does not understand what is going on with you (although they think they do). I will speak briefly of the behavioural and emotional characteristics of a teenager before I then move on to discuss why you are who you are and by that I mean the person you have grown to become.

Characteristics of Adolescence

Adolescents come to have opinions and beliefs that their opinions are the best and that things can work their way. Sometimes, they hardly want to accept opinions or observations that oppose their own ideas. Their inability to believe other persons is based on their lack of experience to support their own beliefs.

The Adolescent wants to attach to someone they think they like at this stage. This person could be a person of the same sex or of the other sex, a friend, teacher, a family member or relatives. The book *Junior Secondary Home Economics*[1] shares some thoughts about Adolescence.

Search for independence from Adults

Adolescents see themselves as adults and want their own freedom and of course the parents at this period see the adolescent as not being able to handle that freedom just yet, so they refuse to grant independence to the adolescent. The adult's unwillingness to grant freedom puts some pressure on the youths and they try to enforce their freedom within their peers. Hence they move together in cliques and react to situations in gangs. This explains why they prefer the company of their peers to that of adults. The adolescent, whether male or female wants acceptance and approval of their behaviour by other people and since adults would not 'cooperate', they seek for independence amidst their peers.

Adolescents want an ideal and sophisticated life. The physical changes make them search for sophistication as they believe they are mature. Many actions of adolescents in the school at this time are against school rules. There is always a conflict between school rules and adolescent behaviours especially regarding boy-girl relationships, dressing, body care, hair care and other general issues.

Observations have also revealed that Adolescents might prefer social activities to academics. They organize social activities on their own, selecting leaders within themselves. In situations where discipline is weak, they react negatively to academics through noise making, hissing or other anti-social behaviours.

Females have more superficial physical development than their male counterparts which make them interested in males older than they are. They also want more mature forms of interaction with boys than with girls of their age.

This is not to say all adolescents go through all of this all the time, but depending on the environment they grow up in, these characteristics manifest in varying degrees and they self-adjust as the young person begins to leave the teenage years.

Physical Changes during Puberty

While I would like to spare you reading another long text of biology stuffs and maybe 'jargons', I would like to briefly go over what actually happens at puberty on your journey to and in your teenage years. It is believed that the onset of puberty is 10 or 11 years for girls and 11 or 12 years for boys. Accompanying the characteristics mentioned earlier are the physical developmental changes that become very obvious. Depending on your age, you would be going through these changes at one point or the other and sometime long before you clock 13 years old.

Some of these physical changes, as described in a text- *Junior Secondary Home Economics*[1] include:

1. The rapid growth in both sexes. This growth is more rapid in girls between ages 11-13.
2. There is growth of hair in the pubic region and in the armpit.
3. The female voice reduces in pitch and the male voice breaks and becomes deep.
4. The hips of females grow wider and rounded and there is increased growth of the breasts.
5. There might be appearance of skin troubles which include pimples, boils and black spots.
6. There is the start of menstruation (Menarche) in females.

Your Today, Your Future

Adolescence is a very important period of every man or woman's life. It is the bedrock and foundation of the future. The 11-19 and 20-25 age ranges are when you get to mold your life and shape it into what you want amidst every other external factor around you. These external factors include your family influence, education, upbringing and your environment. Though most times, the child before adolescence has no say in any of the external factors but now that you are a teenager, you are a major participant in your life development. The book in your hands is to help position your mindset so you can maximize your personality and the many opportunities available to you at this time. Now that it is not late, you can define, redefine, build, shape and determine your future. And to do that, you need a balanced mental attitude and the right thinking such that no matter the factors and situations around you, you can still create for yourself the right attitude for a bright future. How you were brought up from birth through your infant years and as a young child have defined your personality as a teenager. You should know that whatever you learn and imbibe in your 11-19 age bracket determines who you become and how you behave

The child before adolescence, has no say in any of the external factors but now that you are a teenager, you are a major participant in your life development

in your 20-25 age brackets and this in turn determines your entire future.

Now is the time to lay a good foundation and to build well for a time is coming when some things are set in stone and cannot be changed. Little wonder the youth are always looking ahead into the future with statements like: 'I will', 'I like to', 'I must' and the likes. The adults and aged look back into the past, because they cannot change so much either because they have accomplished their dreams or failed to accomplish them. They are already in their 'future' so all they can do is to look back and comment about their past; 'I can't', 'I used to…', 'I wish I had…', 'If I could…', 'What if…?'

> **Now is the time to lay a good foundation and to build well for a time is coming when some things are set in stone and cannot be changed.**

The way you spend your time today determines your future. Spend your teenage years wisely to ensure you have the right foundation that secures for you a great future. The right mental attitude, the right behaviours, the right habits, the right character and quality time management are qualities you need to begin to develop now. There might be need at this juncture for you to start thinking of changing some habits that are likely to mar your future. You might need a change of character, behaviour, attitudes and thoughts. Your thoughts determine your attitude and your attitude shows your behaviour. Your behaviour then sums up your character. Let us talk about how you came to be who you have become.

The Upbringing

By now of course, you can distinguish different character patterns. Look at the people around you or even your friends, you notice different character traits. Some are quiet and easy going, some talk a lot, some are trouble makers and some are very jovial. The widely accepted temperament classification into choleric, sanguine, melancholy and phlegmatic well explains this idea. However, I will not go into details about those classifications here. What you should however know is that it is the way we were brought up as young children, the environment in which we grew up and the influence of our friends and relatives amidst other factors that determines our behavioral patterns as adolescents and ultimately defines who we are up until this point. It takes learning, unlearning and re-learning, acquiring knowledge, commitment and dedication to defy our backgrounds to become the opposite of what our upbringing defined for us. Note that this redefinition of self can be positive or negative.

Meet some friends

Let's meet 5 new friends. They will help us a lot to understand the idea of upbringing and behaviour and we will look at how we can learn from their experiences.

Richey was born into a wealthy family and he is the last child of his parents and has two elder sisters. His mum owns a large super market and his dad is a chartered accountant. Richey has never learnt to do any house chore because they have stewards who help with all the house chores. The only work left for him to do is to take care of his bedroom: a task he finds so difficult to do as his room is always in a complete mess. His dad gives him all he wants and spends lavishly on him using gifts to appease him every time he cries or whines. Richey has now become extravagant and spends money on irrelevant things at the expense of other more important things. He is proud and does not quite show respect and courtesy to his friends and seniors. His friends are of the opinion that he is a very lazy boy. Presently, he still cannot do basic house chores and he cannot cook a meal, not even a sandwich.

Let us meet Raleigh who does not live with her mother. Her mum had left her dad after they divorced when Raleigh was only three years old. She grew up living with her father and step. Raleigh's dad works far away from home so he comes home only on weekends. She doesn't see much of her dad who also attends to his business for most of the weekend. The step-mother is no help either. She insults Raleigh whenever she makes the slightest mistakes. She calls her names and tells her 'she is good for nothing'. Raleigh goes to school as an unhappy and dejected girl who thinks she is worthless and she doesn't know why the world is so full of hate. She presently does not perform well in class. Actually she performs better than only one person out of a class of thirty-five. It looks like she would never improve and her teachers have given up on her.

Ruth was born to the third wife of a polygamous home. She grew up enjoying watching the wives quarrel and sometimes fight in their family home. The wives use all sorts of abusive and profane languages. Ruth has of course over the years memorized all such abusive languages and she uses them at school on her mates. Ruth now believes that to show your displeasure and anger, it is best to put up a fight and teach the 'offender' a lesson. Those who mistakenly step on her toes or get in her way would get a rain of abuses. Ruth is always happy that no one can stand her at school when it comes to name-calling or in a real fight.

Here is Raphael, his dad never sees anything good in what his wife (Raphael's mum) does. He talks to her disrespectfully in front of the children and complains about almost everything. Raphael cannot count the number of occasions his dad had beat up his mum. He loves his dad anyway as he doesn't let his mum reprimand him when he has done something wrong. He therefore continues to disobey his mum. He hisses and complains as soon as he is sent on an errand. He never cares to show respect to the elderly. Surprisingly, he clamours for respect from his classmates and he bullies them at will. Raphael blames everyone but himself for every wrong thing he does and does not mind beating up anyone who challenges him.

Ramsey's dad and mum spend a lot of their time at home with him. They encourage him to study hard so he can perform excellently in his academics. His parents are able to meet all his needs but they ensure that they do not pamper him with too much. Ramsey has to work hard to earn his gifts either by doing a house chore or doing well in school. His mum does not let the house-help tidy his room so Ramsey has to tidy his room himself and he does this every weekend. Ramsey has learnt to cook and loves baking. He is liked by his neighbours and his friends think he is very intelligent. He performs well in class and is loved by his teachers.

We have met Richey, Raleigh, Ruth, Raphael and Ramsey and we have seen how they behave in and outside their homes. We also have some insight into their home backgrounds. If you would observe closely, you would find out that it was the way and manner that each of them were brought up that determined how they now behave. Being careful not to over-generalize, there would be other factors that have contributed to their behaviours but it is true that their upbringing goes a long way to determine their behaviours and you have probably seen a reflection of yourself or people you know in these stories.

You behave like your dad, your mum, close relatives or like a combination of them picking bits and pieces of characteristics here and there. As you grow from being a toddler to a child and to being an adolescent you consciously and unconsciously learn from your immediate surroundings. You mimic your parents' characters and that of people around you. Aside environmental influence, biology helps us to understand that there are transferrable and heritable traits parents can transfer to their child.

If they were your friends

If you had Richey as a friend and you didn't know his parents, you would wonder why he doesn't think about his future and why he spends money on irrelevant things. You would probably judge that he wastes money. At times you might wish you had as much money and you will start picturing how well you would spend yours. Who do we blame for his behaviours? No, we shouldn't blame him. That was how he was brought up.

For Raleigh, you would always wonder why she is so dull and why she would never get any question right. Of course, you do not know the ordeals she faces at home. She has no one to talk to and school is not helping either because no one wants to be her friend.

'Ruth lacks home training', a lot of people would say. 'She has a sharp tongue and she is too abusive for my liking', some others would comment. You don't want to be her friend and you want to avoid her in every way. Her family has set the pattern for her behaviour and she cannot be anything else outside that until deliberate steps are taken.

The opinion of many is that Ramsey is very gentle and quiet. He doesn't talk much and he is very brilliant. Did Ramsey make himself this way? No it's all about the upbringing. A poem by Dorothy Law Nolte titled *Children Learn What They Live*[2] explains it all.

"If children live with criticism, they learn to condemn
If children live with hostility, they learn to fight.
If children live with ridicule, they learn to be shy.
If children live with shame, they learns to feel guilty
If children live with encouragement, they learn confidence
If children live with tolerance, they learn to be patient
If children live with praise, they learn to appreciate
If children live with acceptance, they learn to love
If children live with approval, they learn to like themselves
If children live with honesty, they learn truthfulness
If children live with security, they learn to have faith in
themselves and others
If children live with friendliness, they learn the world is a nice
place in which to live" - Dorothy Law Nolte

Make the Change

I say it again, your upbringing so far has determined your personality till date, but you do not have to retain your attitudes and behaviours if it is not a lifestyle that will secure a great future. With knowledge like what you are getting from this book, you can make the required changes that would set you up for a brilliant future. Try to do what needs to be done to improve your person. If you get angry easily, make the conscious effort to always suppress your anger and part of that effort is to learn about anger. If you are the unforgiving type, learn to forgive. If you are not too good in caring, giving and helping others, start seeing how you could bless other lives with the little things you have. Just ensure you are getting better day by day.

"Birthplace does not have to become a permanent address" – Ben Carson

Judging Others

Vividly, it can be seen that it is wrong to judge people without hearing them out first. If you usually judge or condemn others without hearing their side of the story, please desist from it. When we judge, we pass a sentence and sometimes our judgments are not true. Imagine you were in the same class with Raleigh, you would have judged that she was a dullard; probably you would even laugh at her when your teacher announces that she scored zero in the test. But you never knew what she was going through at home.

Never judge people, instead seek to understand and accept people. Accept everyone the way they are, seek for ways you could help them improve, and pray for them. This is a very important principle in life and I have used it so often. It makes you at peace with everyone and although you cannot please everybody, you would please 'almost' everybody except those of course who refuse to be pleased. But still, it is your duty to love. Be friendly, be jovial and never be cold towards any person because of who or what they are now and never because of what someone told you about them. It is like rejecting someone before you even meet them.

> **The next time people complain about a particular habit or character of yours, do not just go ahead to give excuses, give it a thought.**

Remember, you can be a victim of other's judgment too as you have your own shortcomings, behaviours and habits that you need to work on. Take a pause; think about your life thus far. How well are you faring in being a person of virtue? What do people say about you? This does not mean what people think about you always matters: we cannot please everybody, but largely, what people think about us does matter. If a lot of people share an opinion about you, then everybody cannot be wrong and there is always an element of truth even in rumours.

Your Problem with People

As a teenager, especially in your late teenage years, you might find it hard to understand why adults and sometimes your parents are always complaining about you. In your opinion, they do not readily appreciate the good things you do but they would always be quick to point out your mistakes. Most teenagers find it difficult to cope with this, especially when they crave that freedom they have been denied so much. Do not always see complaints in a negative light. When people complain about you, take that experience and make it work for you. The next time people complain about a particular habit or character of yours, do not just go ahead to give excuses, and give it a thought. Before you go to bed each day, try to think about what was said and see if there is an element of truth in it. If there is the slightest bit of truth, adjust and work towards making a change. If it is not true, discipline yourself so much that it would never come to be true.

Your Tomorrow

As you grow from being a kid to being a teenager, you are also becoming an adult. Are you looking forward to that time when you will become a parent, an employee, an employer, a wife or a husband? If you are not, then you had better get started. Picture the good life you want for yourself. Dream it, write it down, and never forget it. Remember that the dreams of today are the realities of tomorrow. I love writing a lot and started writing my 'book of memories' which I anticipate will someday become my autobiography. I started writing that before I ever thought of writing this book and I can tell you that all I have achieved so far in my lifetime were already conceived and written down in my 'book of memories' where I also document my dreams and aspirations. Those writings have helped a lot to put my life in perspective.

> **Live your life with deep respect for God.**

You must make sure that you do not do things that would jeopardize your tomorrow. Keep the right friends and let your parents and teachers bring you up in a way that is right, obey instructions, live responsibly and most importantly, live your life with deep respect for God. Live according to his statues and you would find life pleasant to live in because God's Word is the answer to all life's questions.

WORK TO DO #1

♣ What would you say are your strengths and weaknesses?

STRENGHTS

1. _______________________________

2. _______________________________

3. _______________________________

4. _______________________________

5. _______________________________

WEAKNESSES

1. _______________________________

2. _______________________________

3. _______________________________

4. _______________________________

5. _______________________________

♣ Ask your dad, mum and two friends what they think about you and write down your answers.

POSITIVE

1. _______________________________

2. _______________________________

3. _______________________________

4. _______________________________

5. _______________________________

NEGATIVE

____

____

____

____

♣ What do you need to do to improve yourself on each of the weaknesses that have been highlighted

1. _______________________________

2. _______________________________

3 _______________________________

4. _______________________________

5. _______________________________

ACTIVITY #1

From this list below, tick traits you think you have and those you will like to improve on and think of how you can achieve these goals.

Adaptable	Skillful	Leader	Entertaining
Reliable	Speaker	Dexterous	Imaginative
Energetic	Confident	Teacher	Artistic
Articulate	Athletic	Trustworthy	Optimistic
Reliable	Spiritual	Visionary	Practical
Committed	Generous	Kind	Write
Fun	Honesty	Responsible	Ambitious

TEEN FOCUS #2
YOU & YOUR HOME

A wise child accepts his parents discipline, a mocker refuses to listen to correction- Prov. 13: 1

There is probably nothing I want to tell you about your family that you do not already know (and hey! how am I supposed to know?). That is not the aim of this Teen Focus. However, I hope you can gain a lot of insight into how to relate better with your family members and be a blessing to them.

There is a definite purpose why you were born into your specific family and not in another. God chose your dad and mum to be your parents for a reason. You had no hand in the decision making. Your parents were given to you as a gift as much as you were given to them as a gift- learn to love, respect and appreciate them. Growing up in a family has its privileges. Likewise, it has its many responsibilities. It is up to you to discover your role in the family so you can make your own contribution to its growth, wholeness and togetherness.

Your home is your basic security; they are always there for you especially when you need help. Love them and make your own valuable contribution to your family. If you don't, you will be a sort of parasite who only wants to get and never give.

Things Get Different

As you progress up the teenage years, you probably notice that things start getting different. It might seem that your parents are 'ganging up' against you and even your siblings are not cooperating either. You might find it difficult to please them as they usually find a fault in everything you do. This is generally a normal experience most adolescent face. In Teen Focus #1, I talked about the changes at puberty which gives teens the feeling that they are now grown enough to make decisions for themselves. You want some freedom but it seems like they would not let you have it any way.

Could They Hate You?

What words can describe how you feel towards your parents if it seems like they are giving you a hard time? At this stage, you just want to be free but you don't understand why they would not even give you a chance to prove yourself. I would say this is a period for you to learn patience and understanding, so see it as an opportunity. Your parents do love you: you know they do. You only need to learn to play your part as a younger member of the family and learn to be obedient and submissive. A Yoruba proverb explains that, 'what an aged man sees sitting, a young child would not see standing up'. You need to trust the wisdom of your parents to lead and guide you right.

You Need Positive Influences

Your parents and siblings all play an important role in influencing you. These influences might be positive or negative. Your parents' duty is to influence you positively, but in reality, it might be otherwise. As a young person, you should be wary of negative influences and try your best not to let them get to you.

Positive activities that influence teenagers include: honesty, home care, cooperation, protecting one another, hard work, meeting family needs, cooking meals and sharing, to mention a few. Negative influences could include smoking, drinking, stealing, laziness, gossiping, unnecessary extravagance, telling lies, quarrelling and late nights.

Praise George shares some thoughts in his book, *Rules for Teens*[1] and I will share some of them with you

Important Notes for Teens

♥ You must learn to take on the burden of responsibility if you want to be treated with respect by your parents and siblings. Maturity has nothing to do with how old you are. It is actually the acceptance of responsibility.

♥ Respect the personal space and property of your parents and that of other family members.

♥ Learn to accept the members of your family for who they are and learn to forgive them though you would be misunderstood, irritated and offended by them. You cannot afford to lodge hatred and bitterness in your heart. You should therefore deal with your negative feelings by prayer. Also learn to talk issues over with persons concerned.

♥ Honour your father and mother and obey them. If you want God's blessings on your life, keep to their instructions. Love and respect them though they are not perfect. It is rebellion against God to be disobedient in any form and for whatever reason.

♥ Report any case of physical, sexual or emotional abuse you may experience. Never hide them. You can report to your parents or Teacher or to any other adult you can trust. Never agree to keep silent about an abusive behaviour to you or any of your siblings. Tell someone trustworthy.

♥ You need to learn to discuss issues that bother you with your parents because they have more experience in life than you or your friends have. From them you get mature and wise advice which will save you from lots of trouble.

♥ You are responsible to protect the integrity of your family; support and stand with your family members in times of crisis and difficulty. Also learn to celebrate their victories and joys.

- ♥ Remember, one day you will have your own family. Be a blessing to your parents and siblings and treat them as you would like your own children to treat you
- ♥ Be eager to make a contribution to the upkeep of your household Complete your household chores without being forced, coerced or punished.

WORK TO DO #2

♣ What activities or attitudes of your parents do you think has influenced or can influence you?

POSITIVE

1.
____
2.
____
3.
____
4.
____
5.
____

NEGATIVE

1.
____
2.
____
3.
____
4.
____
5.
____

♣ What activities or attitudes of your siblings do you think has influenced you or can influence you?

POSITIVE

1.
____
2.
____
3.
____
4.
____
5.
____

NEGATIVE

1.

2.

3.

4.

5.

♣ What are your roles or tasks in your house that you are expected to do?

1.

2.

3.

4.

5.

ACTIVITY #2

Discuss with your parents and siblings about you wanting to improve on your weakness and your desire to stop you bad habits. Let them give you valuable suggestions and tell them to help monitor your progress.

This page was intentionally left blank

TEEN FOCUS #3
YOU & YOUR FUTURE

A wise youth harvests in the summer; but one who sleeps during
harvest is a disgrace-   Prov. 10: 5

This Teen Focus borders on things you should give
thought to in order to prepare yourself for a great future. As
a teenager, you have most of your life ahead of you and you
need to begin to think about how to proactively chart your
course in life to achieve your lofty dreams.

In a couple of years, you will most likely not have
your parents around to make any decision for you. Not too
long from now, though it looks like ages, you would have
all the freedom you always wanted.
What do you think you would do with
this freedom? You probably cannot wait
to get into university far away from
home and you maybe dreaming of doing
the things they never let you do at home.
I must say that freedom is good but
'freedom' is not lack of self-control. You would need to
learn to manage freedom if you want to make the most of
your life and have a fulfilling future.

What Are Your Dreams?

What do you see yourself accomplishing in the
future, what kind of home, family and job do you want?

Which dreams are you conceiving? What do you want for yourself? These questions all seem to be asking the same thing and indeed they beg your answers. You should not just live your life anyhow, accepting whatever comes your way. You should have an insight into what kind of future you want for yourself and be proactive about making that dream a reality. I have learnt from Zig Ziglar that to achieve superior results, I should ensure my successes are not mere accidents; but that I should be involved in the process[1].He also notes that 'everyone has to make a decision: a determination of what he or she wants to achieve in the future'[2].If this is a place you have not come to before now, you need to take time to think about it. If necessary, drop the book for a few minutes.

> **When you celebrate your 50th birthday, what do you want to have achieved in your lifetime?**

It does not matter where you have been, what you have been through and whatever your present situation is. Picture a clean slate before you, a clean slate on which to write, and draw if you would, the future of your dreams. I dare you to dream big. You only need to dream it, desire it, and put it into writing and with the right actions and choices, that dream would be a reality sooner than you think.

When you celebrate your 50th birthday, what do you want to have achieved in your lifetime and what impact do you want to have made on the world? Think beyond wishing and dreaming that you would be the richest man in your country or in the world. That looks more like a selfish dream and the scriptures advise that fulfillment in life is not defined by the wealth and material riches one has.[3]Close your eyes, dream, what do you see?

*"Change will not come if we wait for some
other person or some other time. We are the
ones we've been waiting for. We are the change
that we seek"* – Barrack Obama

What are your dreams? Are these on the list; a happy home, a wonderful spouse, obedient and God-fearing children, a healthy family, a source of blessing to your generation, much comfort and security, great wealth, becoming a solution provider, an innovator? Are these what you desire for yourself or you would rather prefer a troubled home with an unfaithful spouse, insecurity, rebellious children, and the likes? What do you want? Take a few minutes to ponder over this question and to answer it. I suggest you put your answers down into your notepad.

Dream big, work hard, never give in, never give up. One day at a time, one step at a time, until your dream becomes your reality and your reality becomes your dream

One of my life's resolve, documented in my 'book of

memories' is 'Dream big, work hard, never give in, never give up. One day at a time, one step at a time, until your dream becomes your reality and your reality becomes your dream'. This book in your hands is one of those dreams I did not give up on.

Make Your Choices

Are you serious about the picture of the future that you are painting? I am making a general assumption that it is definitely a good picture you have painted in your mind. Now I want to ask, are you sure that is what you really want? If you think you are, then you need to be ready to make the choices that would materialize that picture you have painted. You need to make the choices that would make your dreams come true. Being willing and ready to make the right choices reflects whether you are serious about your dreams or not.

You have your life to live and you bear the major consequences of your actions depending on the choices you make

If you are serious about your lofty dreams, you cannot afford to make choices that would jeopardize that future or land you on the other side of your intended destination. In any case, it becomes important that you evaluate your value system. Your value system is the standards that determine the choices you make. It is always about your values and it is always about your choices. Will keeping bad company of friends help you realize the dream you have set before yourself or moving with friends who are God-fearing? Will engaging in pre-marital sex despite all the dangers help you realize the dream you've set before yourself or preserving your dignity for that wonderful person you would get married to?

"Every choice you make has an end result" - Zig Ziglar

Know that you cannot deceive yourself even if you deceive any other person. You have your life to live and you bear the major consequences of your actions depending on the choices you make. You cannot dream a lofty future and then make negative choices. It does not work that way. Remember! You will reap whatever you sow.[4] So I ask you again. Are you determined to carve for yourself a future that guarantees happiness, joy and fulfillment? Your determination will propel you to always make the right choice every time you have an option to do right or wrong.

Have the Right Values

The choices you make are dependent on the values you have, your beliefs and your ideologies. Likewise, your values are defined by the information and knowledge you have imbibed. I believe Teen Focus #1 has been able to shed light on the fact that you might need to make some necessary changes in your thinking and mental attitude.

This is more or less making the changes to ensure you have values that are right and that produce good fruits in your behaviour and character. You can take deliberate caution and make up your mind to not let negative factors get at you even if the negative influences are right inside your home, in school or in the neighbourhood.

No matter how hard parents try, the bottom line is that it is up to you to make a choice. Identify all areas where you need to make those changes in your values, and beliefs and then make those changes. Remember, it is a matter of choice. I ask again and I ask again, what future do you want for yourself?

Break down Dreams into Goals

Learn the habit of breaking down your dreams into short term and long term goals. Ask yourself, what can I do each day that would make me a better person and help me achieve my goals? By now, you should know I am an advocate of always writing everything down. Set 'smart' goals and you are on your way to that future you can picture.

*"The discipline you learn and character you build
from setting and achieving a goal can be more
valuable than the achievement of the goal itself"* –
Bo Bennett

Spend Your Time Wisely

Let's face it, we are in the 21st century; the world has been reduced to a global village. The world has gone supposedly more social (online) but really less social (face-to-face). I remember only opening my first email account in 2002when I was in my 5th year of college (S.S 2) at age 15. I would have been considered to be an early bird back then. To give you a picture, Yahoo mail launched in 1994, Facebook was founded in 2004, and Gmail was launched by Google in 2004. The trend is not the same anymore as 13 year olds can now and have now registered on social networks.

The social media and internet is good for many reasons. It breaks down terrestrial borders and social class boundaries. You do not have to be somewhere physically to learn about a place or a thing, neither do you have to be rich or wealthy to have access to information. You can live in village that does not exist on a map and still access the whole world from there. Interestingly, there is almost no information you cannot find online. Google has done so well to build their brand that currently, we say less of 'have you searched online?' instead; we say 'have you 'goggled' it?'

You spend a lot of time online and sometimes hours. You also spend a lot of money to pay for access to the internet, but the question I should ask at this point is what do you do online? Chatting away on Facebook, reading up jokes and gossips? Wasting away and killing time on dating or pornographic sites? There are many unproductive activities online and I hope those are not what you engage in. You should be aware that there are also so many productive activities you can engage in online. Learn a new skill or a subject. Share your knowledge and network with like-minded people. Attend school online or join a cause. Whatever you do, spend your time wisely. Do not lose sight of the future you painted and always ask yourself if your activities online will give you that future.

Brian Tracy in his book *Eat that Frog*[5] shares some principles that can help one achieve success in his or her life's pursuit. I will highlight two of them. Firstly, he advises that one should plan every day in advance. Make a plan of your day the night before or early in the morning and arrange them in their order of priority. It helps you to be more productive daily. He also talked about the law of forced efficiency. This means that there is never enough time to do everything but there is always enough time to do the most important things. Find out the most important things to you and do them. Note the things that are important for you to achieve each week and prioritize them.

WORK TO DO #3

♣ Where can you see yourself in the future? What do you see yourself doing and achieving?

____

____

____

____

♣ What activities or attitudes do you need to inculcate to make you become the person you want to be in future?

____

____

____

____

♣ What activities or attitudes do you need to stop or not involve in not to jeopardize your desired future?

____

____

____

____

ACTIVITY #3

a. After doing 'Work To Do' #3, get a sheet of paper and write out your dreams and aspirations. Also write the habits that can help you achieve those dreams. Write down your goals too and paste the paper beside your bed, on your reading table, on your door, or somewhere within your house where you would always see it when you pass.

b. Get a drawing paper and make a drawing titled "The Future of My Dreams". It does not have to be colourful but be creative about it. Put this picture up somewhere you will always see it.

TEEN FOCUS #4
YOU & YOUR EDUCATION

In the same way, wisdom is sweet to your soul. If you find it, you would have a bright future and your hopes would not be cut short-
Prov. 24: 14

A very important part of your existence on this terrestrial globe is your education which is not restricted to learning in the traditional schools. You are reading this book to become a better person, all because you have learnt to read the English language. Education is said to be the best legacy and it truly is. Whether or not you enjoy going to school, whether or not you are being forced to go to school or take any form of education, whether you are sponsored to go to school or you are paying your way through, education is a key element of your life and growth.

Education Is Power

Education is a process of training and instructing to give knowledge and develop skills. It is the totality of knowledge acquisition in any field whatsoever. Knowledge in this regard is just about anything. Education gives you an edge over others who do not know what you have learnt, and it always works out that they might have to pay you for their ignorance. Every time you have ever paid money for a product or service, it is because that person has a knowledge which you do not have. Education is power.

Education is not just about going to school, it includes learning to draw, learning to paint, learning to make beads, to sew clothes, learning a language, learning to be a scientist, economist, artist and the list goes on and on. Basically, having knowledge about a certain field or about a certain topic means being educated in that field. Someone not educated in that field or topic sees you as the 'learned one' or the 'expert' anytime a discussion about that field is raised. There are different types of education and I will mention them briefly.

Informal Education

This is all the education, information, and knowledge you get outside the four walls of a classroom. It is in itself a wide branch of learning, because every education outside the traditional school falls in this category. What are the things you have learnt outside school and probably in school during extracurricular activities? Every one of them is entirely a form of education. Note that Informal education includes:

- Lessons from home (moral, hygiene, house chores and so on)
- Lessons from friends and people around
- From social gatherings and associations
- Hobbies and sport you are involved in.
- Lessons from Nature and the surroundings

Be informed about what's going on in the news. Ask questions whenever you have the opportunity to. Do not hesitate to ask questions to satisfy your curiosity and if you think you are not the curious type, a little curiosity will be helpful. You only get answers when you ask questions and only then do you gain knowledge which would of course make you a better person if applied with wisdom. The Internet on its own is a gateway to a wealth of knowledge. Surf the internet and carry out research to know what's happening around the globe. Do not waste all of your time chatting on the social media platforms without getting any tangible benefit.

Read biographies of successful people, read educational books that interest you, attend workshops and seminars, interact with elders and leaders in your community. Do these and you are poised to affect the world positively. Zig Ziglar in his book, *You can reach the Top*[1] reported that more than half of the people in a society never read another meaningful book after they left school. He noted that those who make the who's who in the world read an average of 20 meaningful books in a year. Not only does this give them information, but it also provides inspiration which keeps them on the go.

A World Changer

Do you know Ben Carson, the first black Neurosurgeon? He is a professor of neurosurgery, oncology, pediatrics and plastic surgery who has dared to perform surgeries no one in the world was willing to do. He became the first neurosurgeon to separate conjoined twins joined at the head. Ben shares his experience growing up in his books, *Gifted Hands*[2] and *Think Big*[3]. His uneducated mother contributed to his success in a great way and Dr. Ben has himself said this, time and time again. While they were in college, she would force young Ben and his elder brother to go to the community library and read at least two books in a week and she made them to submit a report of what they have read. Unknown to Ben, his mum could not read nor write and she kept it a secret and encouraged her children to study hard.

Visiting the library frequently helped Ben to decipher his interest in the sciences and that was the beginning of his scientific and medical career. He has written six books all of which are best sellers. His first was his autobiography which was published when he was only about 39 years old. Long before he clocked 40, he founded a scholarship fund for outstanding students in America and has taken interest in speaking to teenagers and college students across the world to help them develop the potential within them. Dr. Ben Carson travels wide and has been a positive influence and role model to many, me inclusive. Though now retired, he is seeking the republican nomination to contesting the 2016 US presidential elections. If you like his success story and want others to read about yours, then you should be ready to pay the price.

"Here is the treasure chest of the world – the
public library, or a bookstore."- Ben Carson

It will be worth everything to believe him. Great men who have passed on gave us books to let us into their minds. Reading is not the norm in today's busy society but reading empowers. You as a teen might even have grown up not appreciating the importance of reading. People no longer read books as the reading culture has been thrown to the winds especially in this part of the world. You could count how many libraries we have in a state on the tip of your fingers and fewer people take time to read a meaningful book. Hope you get the message. You have to develop yourself; your skills and talents. Education outside classroom would help you with that.

Reading Books Changed my Life

The year 2000 was a turning point in my life. I had finished my 3rd year of college (J.S.S 3) and had finished the Junior School Certificate Examination. If I passed well, I would move on to the Senior Secondary School but it took a while to get the results of the examination. I was therefore at home for more than three months 'doing nothing'. As if that was not enough, I was always 'home alone 'having the whole house to myself from 7a.m till about 3p.m when my siblings usually returned from school. Here is the real gist. What is a 13 year-old supposed to do with 8 hours all to himself every day for 3 months with a dysfunctional TV and no game console? To add to the list, I had no smart phone and, the power supply to the house was erratic because the power supply company (NEPA) at that time was very inefficient. We were more or less cut off from the power grid. That eliminates many things from the list of what I could be doing at home all by myself.

As if it cannot get worse, my instructions were to not leave the house. Thankfully, I had access to my mum's room. What is there to be thankful for? My mum's library of books was my consolation. That was my solace. My mum, a teacher, majored in English and Literature so she had numerous books; African and non-African authors; The African Child, Things Fall apart, The Concubine, No Longer at Ease, The God's are Not To Blame, Robinson Crusoe, A Tale of Two Cities; you name it. What's more? She had the entire Shakespeare collection.

Day and night, I buried myself into the books eventually reading some of them more than twice. That period of my life exposed me to so much I cannot quantify. I became versed about a lot of things I read in books, and my curiosity and creativity were sparked. My understanding of the English language also received a boost. I became one of the best students in English language all through my 3 year studies at the senior school. Reflecting on all that now, it shouldn't be a surprise that I was one of the best. Reading made all the difference in my life at a time when I could have engaged in evil vices or slipped into depression.

Grab every good opportunity that comes your way to learn something new. When I had the opportunity, I learnt to play the piano, play chess, paint and make crafts. By my final year in college, I was already making money as other students pay me to make them handcrafted greeting cards. I also went on to learn about computers and moved a bit further into graphics design. I went on to learn to play the saxophone (I did not get to far with this) and though I really wanted to learn to dance I never had the opportunity until my final year in the university when I joined a dance group and learnt to dance hip hop and the basics of salsa. All of these were at different time points in my life but they helped me to fully explore my abilities and develop my talents. You can develop yours too. You only need to be thirsty for knowledge and self-development.

"To every man there comes in his life a time, that special moment when he is figuratively tapped on the shoulder and offered a chance to do a very special thing unique to him and fitted to his talent, what a tragedy if that moment finds him unprepared or unqualified for the work which would be his finest hour." – Winston Churchill

I remember a time while I was an undergraduate at the university, probably in my 2nd year. I had exams approaching and went to the library to read up some notes. I later needed to pick up a book on the shelf so I went to the bookshelf and tried to pick out the particular book. While there, I caught sight of the encyclopedia section just adjacent where I stood. I walked over and picked one of the volumes. That was the first time I carried a paperback encyclopedia in my hands. My eyes popped out as I could not but marvel at the richness of information inside it. It was not surprising that I spent the rest of the day reading page after page of the encyclopedia and totally ignored my course work. Till date, I still remember what I read about colours, design and Interior decoration. After that first time, I was hooked. Trips to the library were no longer to read up on course work but to read about anything that catches my interest. I must say this helped me a lot to gain a vast knowledge about a lot of things and fields in the sciences and arts.

My drive to pick up so many skills was part of my desire to be versed and well informed. I have now grown up to become a multi-skilled person and I can rewrite that popular phrase to suit my personality as 'Jack of all trades, master of some'. Current trends inform that at least one should know a little about almost everything even if it is the faintest idea. It is always better than being a complete novice. However, to succeed and stand out, one will need to be a master in at least one field of interest.

Classroom Education

This has to do with the school, teachers, lectures, home works, projects, practical and all sorts. You need to have a real desire to be educated. It's not going to be easy going through High school or university with no strong desire. Sure you want to make the best out of schooling and pass with excellent grades.

Finding it Difficult to Cope in School?

Maybe, you love to go to school but probably find your courses and subjects difficult or you just can't cope with the pressures. At one point or the other, we have all had to face challenges in school. If it is not with the Geography teacher who seems to be a slow talker then it would be with the Mathematics tutor who is just too fast for you to keep up with. If it's not the Biology tutor who gives too much lecture notes, it would be the History class that is so long and boring. My advice to you is to look beyond the brick walls, beyond the challenges on your part and shortcomings on the part of your teachers so you can make the best out of your academics. If someone does not particularly enjoy a subject, let's say physics, physics takes the back sit in that person's private study and such a person would hardly study physics. The person's undoing would be revealed when that person has to sit for physics in the final college examinations.

Why run away cowardly from something you will eventually face head on? Your History tutor is very boring and because of that you have decided to 'hate' History.

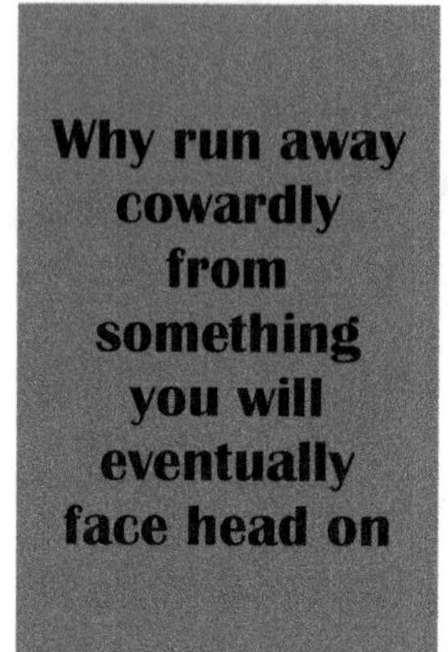

Never forget that you would need to pass History to further your education in the social sciences, the same goes for the sciences. You cannot afford not to like every of your subjects.

There is this younger relative of mine who had no liking for Mathematics. We used to force him to study Mathematics though he was very good in the social sciences subjects. He did not even seem to appreciate the fact that his parents got a private mathematics tutor for him to take him extra classes. Not passing mathematics in his final senior secondary examinations (WASSCE) cost him three years at home, without admission offers at any university. If he had taken mathematics more seriously, He would probably have passed in one attempt. I share this story so you can learn a lesson and not fall into the same situation. All subjects and courses are important. Face them squarely and with dedication.

You can be the Best Student

Yes! You can. Never write yourself off that you cannot be the best in your class. You can be the best if only you would be prepared to take up the challenge. I will share with you some tips necessary for academic excellence from the book *The Insider's Guide to University Success*[4] written by Kehinde Odeniyi, a university lecturer who inspired me a lot during my undergraduate studies. These 'tips' are referred to as the 'Golden Rules of Success' by one of my spiritual mentors, Professor J.K. Oloke. These principles will go a long way to prepare you for academic excellence. They are principles I have practiced myself and got results.

Tips for Academic Excellence

1.   **Know Yourself.** In your quest for academic success, two questions are important. What is your dominant learning style and what part of the day are you most active? Are you the verbal learner who finds easy expression in writing and in speech? You love mnemonics and rhymes or the visual learner who prefers images, pictures, maps and charts to organize information? Also there is the logical learning style that involves using the brain for mathematical and logical reasoning. The physical learner resorts to the use of body language and sense of touch to learn the world around him. We also have the solitary learners and the social learners. Some people learn better when alone and in contrast, there are others who assimilate better when in a group. Know yourself.

2.   **Attend all Classes.** That means exactly what it says. Attend all classes. You get about 70% understanding of the

topic at hand when you attend the lectures in person and listen first-hand.

3.   Write Your Notes Yourself. Ensure you do not let others write your notes for you. Write your notes yourself. You learn and get more understanding as you write, spell and repeat the words in the lecture material or notes. My personal experience was that I did not perform excellently in my pre-degree science programme, although I passed. After I evaluated my performance, I realized that I did better in subjects which I had notes for. Notes I wrote in my own handwriting. I did not do so well in the subjects and courses which had majorly printed course materials (handouts). I resumed the pre-degree program late and had to photocopy notes of the classes which I had missed. It is surprising to know that there were areas in the handouts I never took good notice of, and didn't know were covered in the course until the examinations arrived and I had a handful of questions I could not answer. I do not mean to say everyone will not assimilate well if reading from other people's notes, but for me, it was a factor which determined my performance. Know thyself.

4.   Revise Your Notes Daily. With much ease, you would master your subjects if you would go over all that you were taught in school every day. At the end of the week, take time to go over all the work done during that week and I tell you that you are on your path to an excellent performance in the examinations.

5. **Have a Positive Classroom presence.** Never arrive to class late and do not pass vicious side comments during classes. These only give you a negative classroom presence. Actively participate in the classroom discussion and relate well with your teachers. Kehinde added that a positive classroom presence will give you goodwill with teachers.

> *"Students with a high positive classroom presence might not always have the best results but both staff and students would reckon with them first before brilliant students with a negative or no classroom presence." – Kehinde Odeniyi*

If you want a fulfilling future, concentrate on your Academics. Don't study just to pass, study to gain knowledge and you will get better grades together with the knowledge- that is winning on both ends.

Watch What You Read

There is no bad or good knowledge. Knowledge is knowledge. What matters is what you do with the knowledge you have gotten. Earlier, I talked about education outside the classroom which you get from watching TV, reading magazines, novels, brochures, surfing the internet and asking questions. However, it is important to note that whatever you read and how you use the knowledge affects you positively or negatively. The information you acquire and the people you move with can make or mar you. Wise King Solomon left us with these words, "do not be fooled by those who say such things, bad company corrupts good character"[5].

Reading books and gaining knowledge is like having an interaction with the author or speaker who is the source of what you are reading, watching or hearing.

"When one reads good books, it is like having a conversation with men of breeding who lived in the past."- Rene Descartes

Reading books lets us into the minds of the authors. It automatically takes us to the places they have been and helps us share in the experience they have had. However, not all writers are worth conversing with because not all writers have noble thoughts. You must be selective of the books you read and the movies you watch. Learn to analyze and weigh what you read with the high moral standards-God's own standards. Do not accept unquestioningly everything you read or hear. It is a fact that all humans are susceptible to a certain amount of bias and always speak from their own perspective. Just like the Indian tale of the blind men who were asked to describe an elephant while touching different parts of its body. Some people infact, are not always totally honest in their portrayal of facts.

WORK TO DO #4

♣ Are you finding any of your school subjects difficult to cope with? If yes list them below and write why?

SUBJECT | POSSIBLE REASON

1.

2.

3.

4.

5.

♣ What do you think you need to start doing to improve your performance in each subject?

1.

2.

3.

4.

5.

ACTIVITY #4

a. Discuss with your teacher about your challenges in the subject and ask for their advice on how you can have a better understanding of the subject and how you can improve in your performance. Do not be afraid to approach them, I am sure they would be willing to help if you approach them with courtesy.

b. Try to find books that can help you improve on your weaknesses as you have stated in TEEN FOCUS #1. If you are struggling to figure out books yourself, ask an elder to recommend books to you.

c. Talking about goal setting, you might also want to set a deadline to finish the book. Ensure you give enough time for this. It is not a book to be rushed

BONUS ACTIVITY

Just because this Teen Focus talks about learning, here is a bonus activity.

Write out at least 20 new words from this Teen Focus. Use a dictionary to find their meanings and note them in your book. It will be awesome to see you do this throughout the remainder of the book.

Good Luck with learning new words.

YOU & YOUR FRIENDS

Don't be selfish; don't try to impress others. Be humble, thinking of others as better than yourselves -Phil 2:3

We all agree that no tree can make a forest. Likewise no single person can make a community. God designed mankind in such a way that we are not meant to be 'lone rangers'. We want people around us, we want to love and to feel loved and you are no exception. I am sure you have quite a number of friends around you already; it is just about time we looked at who they are and what value you add to one another.

Handling Relationships

As you relate with and meet more people in school, at home, at church, at the extra classes, at tutorials and even at parties, you are getting to find out that the world is made up of different kinds of people-people of different minds, thoughts, behaviours and attitudes.

You find quite a number of people who are aggressive and you find others who are so gentle. If anyone is like me, you can manage to have a piece of cake in your mouth for a day or two with the cake intact(*don't actually try this with me*).You have some friends who talk so much while some others won't blurt out a word even if you step on their toes. The list is endless from being bold and brave to being shy and timid, and from being expressive to being reserved. Gentility, meekness, impatience, pride, humility and respect are some qualities that individuals possess which makes each person different.

> It is probably impossible to please everybody but it is possible to be at peace with everyone, at least from your own end

Sometimes, life gets very unpleasant because some people have characters that are somewhat bad and they hurt you. Some have no intention of hurting you and others don't just care if you get hurt as long as they have it their way. There is however the need to be at peace with everyone. How do you handle relationships and be at peace with everyone"? It is probably impossible to please everybody but it is possible to be at peace with everyone, at least from your own end.

Understanding People

In Teen Focus #1, I discussed understanding people from the upbringing perspective in details. You could go over it again for a few minutes. When we have evaluated and understood the behaviours of people we have around us, we should then come to accept them just the way they are. Accepting people's flaws is important and necessary if we will live peaceably with them. If we really can accept people the way they are then we would pick offences less frequently if at all. This is because we would have learnt to overlook those faults. This is not to say we cannot and should not correct another person. When you get the opportunity and at an appropriate time, you should let others know when they have offended you and this must be done in love, using good communication skills that describe the action and how it made you feel; not passing judgment and pointing fingers.

For example say, "on that morning, when you stepped on my feet and did not apologise, I felt bad and unhappy that you do not value me as a person. I am not happy about this and I want to let you know how I felt". This kind of response is likely to produce some result and mend the relationship between you both. You might even find out that the person did not take notice of stepping on you. It is better than saying "Are you blind and stupid? Did you not notice that you stepped on me the other day?" This will definitely cause rancor between people and breed feelings which break relationships.

The *Book of Hope*[1] advices that to live in peace with people, we need to:

- ♥ Understand them
- ♥ Accept them for who they are
- ♥ Correct them politely always
- ♥ Endure their characters with patience but

♥   Never join them if it is a wrong act.

Ensure that although you accept people's shortcomings and weaknesses, you do not join them in the negative behaviours. It is common to see people tolerate some behaviours of their friends and before long, they join them because they no longer see anything wrong with that particular behaviour after spending a lot of time around, long enough to become familiar with it. Sadly, some move quickly from the place of tolerance to acceptance, then to getting involved and before long, they begin to enjoy doing that negative habit they had detested initially. It is surprising to even note that sometimes, the newbie end up worse than the person who introduced the negative habit in the first place. Be on your guard.

Friendships

If you are in trouble or facing a difficult situation, who would you talk to first, your teacher or your parent? Most teenagers talk to friends. Who is a friend? Do you have best friends, or you just keep many close friends? Friendship can be defined as a relationship we have with people we are acquainted with but who are not members of our family. It could fall into various categories.

Casual Friends

They are the faces we recognize and people we greet by name. We see them around occasionally or every other day. In casual friendship, you only tend to greet when you cross path or have contact.

Close Friendships

They are the friends you have kept due to spending time together in one form or the other and with whom you share common interests. You don't really know someone until you have spent time together discussing. When you spend time with a casual friend, if you get to really talk for quite some time and then maybe you then find out that you both have a common interest and views on some particular topics, you begin to get more interested in the person and like each other more and more. There are certain limits in close friendships.

Intimate Friendships

This is the next phase as you get to find so much interest in this person, you think the person understands you and always listens to you. You spend even more time together and you share a lot in common. You discuss a lot about yourselves- your pasts, present and future. You begin to talk about almost anything. Intimate friends always listen to you and are interested in your well-being. You always visit each other, not minding what it costs you to do so. You just want to always be with the other person. However, you can have more than one intimate friend.

Your intimate friend can be of either sexes but I quickly need to say this at this point, if your intimate friend is of the other sex, never be in a hurry to assume that you are in love. Most times when you spend so much time with a particular person of the opposite sex, especially someone worthy of admiration, a feeling creeps within you which could be misinterpreted for 'love'. Be wary. More about this is in explained in Teen Focus #6.

> **If your intimate friend is of the other sex, never be in a hurry to assume that you are in love.**

Everyone desires Intimate friendships; a friend who would accept you the way you are, always watch your back, and stay with you no matter what. A friend that always tells you the truth, a friend interested in your well-being, a friend in need and a friend in deed.

There are two other types of friendships or relationships I would like to mention but they are obviously meant for adults who are ready for marriage. As a teen, you are becoming mature- and not already fully mature. These two types of friendships should not likely be your priorities at this time.

Courtship

For the purpose of this section, I will interchange the use of the two words, 'courtship' and 'engagement'. This type of friendship arises when someone mature and ready for marriage finds someone he or she loves and is ready to make a lifetime commitment with. Love in marriage is not a fantasy, nor a feeling. It is a lifetime commitment between two people. The courtship or engagement period is the period when you get to know much more about that person of the opposite sex, getting to know the characters and habits so you can learn to live with such a person in understanding. It is at this time that you know if you are making the right decision about your marriage; whether it is safe and wise to go ahead into marriage with that person.

In my opinion, you cannot succeed at courting someone who has not passed through the other stages of friendship I mentioned earlier. For adults ready for marriage, passing through all the stages of friendship does not need to take ages. It can be short, but long enough for love to grow. Love grows over time, never forget that. You should only have one person you are in this type of relationship with. There are some things that intimate friends of the opposite sex might not know about you but someone you are engaged to should know them, as you do not want to keep some secrets that might jeopardize the marriage in the future. However, there are still boundaries and limits. The major boundary which should not be compromised is involving in sex and other sexual activities.

Remember, Courtship & Engagement is meant for mature minds. Those who are matured in the five important areas namely:
1. Spiritually
2. Emotionally
3. Mentally
4. Physically
5. Financially

Marriage

> **Never marry because of beauty, looks, wealth, stature or physique, they can fade away with time**

This is of course the peak of relationships between a man and a woman. Marriage is honourable. It is God's own idea that a man should not live all by himself but should have a companion suitable for him.[2] Marriage is sharing your life with someone you have resolved to love every day of your life unconditionally. Marriage is a lifetime school you will not graduate from and it should not be rushed into. According to God's design and intent, once you get into it, there is no going back.

Never marry because of beauty, looks, wealth, stature or physique; they can fade away with time. Any of these can disappear any day and would no longer be there. Beauty would fade, and accidents could cause physical deformities. Marry alone because of true love and wait until you are ready to make a commitment. I will leave more discourse on this for Teen Focus #6

Your Friends- They Make or Mar You

I talked about upbringing in Teen Focus #1 and about how you have come to form your personality based on the upbringing you have. Your teachers in school and your friends also take part in this growing up process. Depending on the type of friends you keep, they can either make you or break you. It is a proven fact that teenagers often believe what friends tell them, and sometimes at the expense of their parents opinion.

Many teenagers and young people feel that their parents are hiding something from them so they approach friends for advice. The unfortunate thing will be approaching a 'bad' friend for advice as that guarantees a 'bad' advice. Your friends always influence you either positively or negatively. Which friends do you keep? There are friends who add value to your life and there are others who might want to diminish the value you have placed on yourself. Dear Teen, your today determines your future, having the wrong set of friends around you will not take you anywhere close to that beautiful future you desire for yourself.

You Can Pick your Friends

You can pick your friends. Yes that's the way it should be. No friend can force himself or herself on you. It is your responsibility to ensure that you pick the right friends that would influence you positively. An edition of the *Vertical Thought*[3] magazine shares some guidelines for picking close friends

Advice for picking Close Friends

- Someone who shares your outlook on life that comes from personally knowing the true God.
- Someone who is of a good character and reputation.
- Someone who speaks with kindness and thoughtfulness without cursing or foulness.
- Someone who has an abiding respect for the law and a conscience to obey it.
- Someone who is sexually moral and has true godly wisdom.

♥ Someone who is honest and is willing to tell you directly his or her considered opinion about the issues of the day or about yourself.

♥ Someone who will listen thoughtfully to your considered opinions.

♥ Someone who has a desire and drive to do the right thing.

♥ Someone who respects you as a person and doesn't think of having sex with you.

♥ Someone who refuses to flatter you to get something from you or to use you.

CRITERIA	%	CRITERIA	%
Keeps confidence	89%	Intelligence	59%
Loyalty	88%	Social conscience	49%
Warmth, Affection	82%	Shares Leisure Interest	46%
Supportive	76%	Shares cultural Interest	30%
Frankness	75%	Similar Education	17%
Sense of Humor	74%	Similar Age	10%
Takes time with You	62%	Physical Attraction	9%
Independence	61%	Similar Political Views	8%
Good conversationalist	59%	Similar Professional Interests	8%

The table above, also taken from the magazine points out what others think are important in choosing and keeping close friends. Do you agree with their selections? Choose the right friends and you are on your path to a bright future but wrong friends put you off track.

Having Difficulty Making Friends?

Sometimes, we want people to reach out to us first before we respond. We want others to give out their hand before we take it. We want others to ask for our friendship before we give it. We look at people who are not our friends afar off and conclude that they are not just friendly. If you think you are good enough for others to make friends with, then go on to make friends with others. If you wait for others to come to you, you might lose very valuable friendships that will never happen.

To make friends, stick your hand out, reach out and give others time and you would be surprised how friendly others are. To make friends easily, learn to listen to others and do less talking. Asking questions and listening shows that you are really interested in them. Also, it is also important to keep in touch in any way possible. Giving a compliment is good but it is not about passing insincere comments. Mean every word you say and sincerely love your friends. Choose your friends wisely and when you eventually make friends, keep them.

What Friendship is Not

Making friends is one thing and keeping your friends is another thing entirely. Being a friend comes with its responsibilities. Some believe that their friend should always agree with them whether they are right or wrong. That is not right! They call it being loyal, but that will be a misplaced loyalty. You do not want a friend who is loyal to you but not loyal to the truth.

Mistaken loyalty is one wrong idea regarding friendship. Another wrong idea about friendship is abandonment. In order to keep from agreeing with a friend who is wrong, some abandon their friends. Some other friends flee whenever a problem arises. They seemingly prefer to disappear or pretend not to notice than to deal with what is really happening and speak up. These set of friends are called 'fair-weather' friends. They are willing to be your friends for as long as everything goes well.

Some believe that their friend should always agree with them whether they are right or wrong. That is not right!

However, we do not have to keep up with a friend who intentionally lives contrary to our godly values. It might become necessary to split up. What this means is that we should not end a friendship because a friend with godly standards occasionally has a problem. Under these circumstances, real friends help each other get through and solve any problems but we can end a friendship that is influencing us negatively if this friend is deliberately involving in ungodly behaviours against our own values. Real friends are 'all-weather' friends who will stick with us through life.

The Hard Talk

One of the most difficult aspects of being a true friend is telling a friend that he or she is doing something wrong when they are. If we are honest with ourselves, we know that occasionally we are in need of a little guidance and encouragement to make right decisions. Real friends are people who always tell us the truth- even when the truth is unpleasant. Real friends give us the much needed reality checks to help us evaluate our actions and know when we might be getting it wrong.

There are times when you would need someone to remind you of your resolves and decisions

It is this measure of friendship that identifies those who truly care for us. These are the kinds of friends who are always there for you even when you run into challenging times.

How to Tell a Friend

Assuming you need to tell a friend that he or she is making a wrong decision or choice. Of course, this can happen sooner or later. What can you do to make the message easier for you to deliver and easier for your friend to receive? Here are some helpful tips from *Questions Young People Ask- Answers that Work*[4].

- ♥ Ask God for wisdom
- ♥ Use a normal tone or Voice
- ♥ Be kind
- ♥ Encourage a godly change
- ♥ Offer to help

Be a True Friend, an all-weather friend, whether you are giving or receiving correction. Be committed to your friends and you will get the best out of life because no matter what you have learnt or the height you have attained, you will need someone to support you. There are also times when you would need someone to remind you of your resolves and decisions. Always build relationships you can lean on in the future.

Peer Pressure

Never let friends force you into doing what you never feel like doing, when it is not something of a good, godly and high moral standard. Don't let your friends cloud your mind with immoral values. Take King Solomon's advice "my son, if sinners entice you, turn your back on them!"[5]. Have your own godly values and live by them no matter what. Let your friends know you for what you stand for and never give in when you are lured to do something evil. In the first place, never keep friends who would someday lure you into evil. Remember you can pick your friends.

WORK TO DO #5

♣   In what ways do your close or intimate friends add value to you?

1.

2.

3.

4.

5.

♣   In what ways have you added value to your close or intimate friends?

1.

2.

3.

4.

5.

ACTIVITY #6

For each of your close friends, write down characters of theirs that you want them to improve upon. Go ahead to tell them about it in a polite way giving your advice while commending their strengths.

This page was intentionally left blank

YOU & THE OPPOSITE SEX

Give honour to marriage, and remain faithful to one another in marriage. God will surely judge people who are immoral and those who commit adultery - Heb. 13: 4

There seems to be a lot of fuss about the opposite sex. Actually! There is and it is real. Growing up as a teenager, I remember this feeling I always had, wanting to be around my friends who were girls. I always preferred their company to just hanging out with the boys. I got attracted to a lot of them and wanted to make friends with the new girl in school. I don't think I am alone in this except you tell me you do not have such an experience as a teenager. This is a phenomenon that happens to almost everyone. I know this because I had other friends who were boys who also had the same feeling and I also know this because these friends of mine who were girls also preferred the company of the boys.

I have used the phrases 'friends who were girls' and 'friends who were boys' in a bid to avoid using the words 'girlfriends', 'boyfriends', 'female friends' and 'male friends'. This is because the words have different usage in different climes. Using any of these four words in this book should be taken loosely to mean 'a friend who is a girl' and 'a friend who is a boy.'

Now let me delve a little deeper. The boys cannot seem to get enough of the girls and as for the girls; it appears all the guys are becoming charming princes. It is interesting to note that this phenomenon occurs even through adulthood although in slightly different ways. I will explain this in the subsequent pages.

As a teenager, you have lots of questions about how to deal with the emotions welling up inside you and how to relate with your friends of the opposite sex, but sometimes, there is no one to answer your questions. This Teen Focus attempts to look into the important issues that come to the fore when it comes to relating with the opposite sex.

Self-Appreciation

Now that puberty has been reached, you begin to appreciate yourself. You now think more highly of yourself and you expect others to see you that same way. You might stop doing some things which you were used to doing- things you would now refer to as childish. You are more conscious of how you dress, how you walk and some girls might give up their dolls. Naturally you want to do things that you usually could not do such as carrying heavy objects. You tend to say to yourself, "I am growing up, I am becoming mature, and in fact I think I am already mature." A lot of the motivation to be different comes from a willingness to please the opposite sex. There is this natural attraction and it a phenomenon I describe as the Boy-Girl Tie ™.

The Boy-Girl Tie™

The *Boy-Girl Tie* (B-G tie) is a bond that has eternally existed between the male and female sexes. The *B-G Tie* is a phenomenon described as 'unlike poles attract and like poles repel', among young folks in physics language. As a boy, you often prefer the company of your female friends, and the girls just want to be around the boys and talk for hours unending. Both sexes reach a point where they seem to prefer the company of the opposite sex to friends of the same sex.

The *B-G Tie* is a natural attraction that God put there on purpose. It is not that each sex does not enjoy the company of their same sex friends, they do very much, but there is this physical attraction between the male and the female. Whether at school, in your neighbourhood, or at your religious meetings, there might just be this particular person that you are attracted to or maybe you just like the person because he or she seems to be friendly. Now let's take a deeper look at this *B-G Tie*. Why is it there and how can we make the best use of it?

God's Intended Purpose

God made the earth a lovely place to live in and He created man that he might live and inhabit it. God wants all mankind to live in peace and harmony with one another. This is vivid in the bible account of creation.

> *"God said, we'll make man in our image, they will look like us and have power over the fish, the birds and all animals, domestic and wild, large and small. So God created human beings making them to be like himself. He created them male and female, blessed them and said, "have many children, so that your descendants will live all over the earth and bring it under their control[1]*

God planned marriage (between a man and woman) so that it would produce Godly children who would grow up in an atmosphere of love. How best can God put love in the family- between father, mother and child? This original plan of God will require a deep affection and that was how the B-G Tie was instituted. It was God's own idea.

Enjoying Company

Boys and Girls should enjoy one another's company. In college, you make a lot of friends with whom you share lots of experiences that you want to keep memory of forever. If you are already out of college, cast your mind back to when you were in school. You can probably remember a number of exciting times; talking with friends, pranks on your teachers, nicknames, gossips and all those sorts. A slogan that I have heard so often is 'School life is the best'. You might agree or disagree with that statement but it is not debatable that life in college is one of the coolest things to ever happen to a young person. You enjoy making friends and you really want to meet the new girl who got transferred to your school. These all result from the B-G tie. This tie can cause a lot of trouble for you if you do not understand it and learn to manage it. It can well be misused and this has been the undoing of a lot of youth.

'I Like' Versus 'I Love'

A new girl just got transferred to your school. The first time you saw her you couldn't help gaping and throwing surreptitious glances until she was out of your sight. You were obviously stunned by her striking beauty. There is just something about her, the way she walks, the way she talks, her personality. You can't just put your fingers on what makes you attracted to her. You really look forward to the day you would get to have a conversation with her. 'You would really love to be a friend to someone like her' you say to yourself. You might or might not have had even an opportunity to speak with her yet. If you ever get to become her close friend, you consider it a privilege considering the number of people, both male and female who want to be in her close circle of friends. Does this scenario sound familiar?

You now seem to enjoy her company, you always want to be around her and as you converse with her, do class work together, have class breaks, go for sports and even walk home together, you notice you like a lot of things about her. You are really getting to like her very much. In fact, you begin to think you do love her. 'It's like I'm in love' you might say.

No doubt everyone wants to be loved and accepted. Getting much attention, care and spending a lot of time with a person of the opposite sex makes you feel accepted. Talking about the *B– G Tie*, your emotions are stirred and because you haven't mastered the art of controlling your emotions you make a wrong conclusion that you are in love. The females are not left out as they also get to have this crush on the charming males. That new girl probably spotted the boy from the distance but looked away to avoid eye contact. She was however dying to meet this cute lad. Finally, she did and he is the man of her fantasies.

Having a liking for persons of the opposite sex and appreciating them for being a friend who adds value to you should never be mistaken for erotic love. Never be carried away by what movies, music, T.V adverts and magazines portray. You love everybody and do not hate anybody so there should be no fuss about 'loving 'him or her. Definitely, you love your dad, likewise your mum and your siblings. You love your friends, and families. The person in question is not excluded from this list. You love him or her too. Be careful not to be taken over by Infatuation. Now let's talk about that.

Infatuation

Everybody in many ways is looking for a place where they would be accepted- someone who can accept them despite their flaws. Angelina Pandian is credited with this quote. "For to love and to be loved, is the essence of life", and I cannot agree more. Friendships are therefore a good platform to give and receive love. A lot of movies, music, and books portray heroes falling in love with the fair princess and then they live happily ever after. We can fantasize such for ourselves and we tend to believe that we always have to fall in love. That there always has to be a prince charming or a beautiful damsel in your life, but the brain sometimes fools us all.

Research[2] has shown that the brain's logic center is where love resides. Studies also show that the human brains responds when we meet someone we find attractive. Neurotransmitters such as Dopamine and Serotonin are released. Dopamine creates intense energy and motivation when it is in its right proportions just like Serotonin would do. However a Serotonin imbalance could cause an obsessive compulsive disorder

> **Never be carried away by what the movies, music, T.V adverts and magazines portray**

which could be related to mental instability, except for that it is reflected as an emotional imbalance.

Someone in this position has very strong emotional feelings and different terms are used to describe this state of the mind- 'love sickness', 'passionate love', 'romantic love', 'emotional chemistry', and to use more informal phrases, 'love wantintin' and 'love in Tokyo'. It is this new feeling one has when attracted to the opposite sex; such emotions change over time and is never stable. Falling in and out of love every now and then with different persons can never be true love but Infatuation.

'It was Allen's first day in computer school, he walked into the class, looked around to see if he would see anyone he knew. As he moved his eyes, he saw a girl dressed in a beautiful top and jeans skirt, she was fair skinned and in his judgment, he would say she was beautiful. Allen noticed an empty seat next to her, their eyes met briefly and a sweet smile crossed her face. Allen knew immediately that was all the invitation he needed. They started dating not long after that first day in class. After three months, they had to break up because Allen found out she wasn't the type of person he wanted as a friend, she was dating other guys and was even involved in sex. She lied a lot and wasn't doing well at her studies.

She was dishonest, unfriendly and unkind. Allen could no longer cope.'[3]

What can you make of the story above? The brain deceives us as much as the T.V, movies, soap operas, romantic novels, music and magazines want it to. They cloud us with tales of love that we have been forced to believe the magical 'happily ever after' islands, even though they do not exist.

Love at First Sight, Is It Real?

You cannot love someone you do not know and how can you know someone at first sight? Love develops over time. Love here refers to erotic love. You may be attracted to a person at first sight and your heart may skip a beat or two, yes- but you can definitely not 'fall 'in love with someone at first sight. Except you want to get an injury, then you 'fall in love 'prematurely, but be careful, you might not get out of that ditch and if you do, it won't be without bruises and wounds. Such feelings at first sight isn't real love, it is Infatuation. It is more practicable to 'walk' into love than to 'fall' in it.

Many of the wrong ideas concerning love comes from popular songs, the lyrics to one says "how do I live without you? I want to know...how do I ever survive?"Another one goes like this, "I can see it in your eyes…you are all I've ever wanted…I love you". And another, "I woke up in love today because I went to sleep with you on my mind". The list is endless and if anyone who uses these words ever means them, you should know that it is all but emotional talk, that state of 'emotional imbalance' caused by the disproportionate amounts of neurotransmitters in the brain. What do you make of it, is this really true, that you cannot live another day without another person and that someone else cannot live a day without you? If you have ever been heartbroken from a previous relationship, or you simply ended it, did the skies fall?

Emotions are Unreliable

Emotions and feelings are never stable. They swing from high to low in cycles. When you are in a high swing, you feel great about yourself and you are in a very good mood. A few days later or even minutes later, for no reason at all or due to an event or a misunderstanding, you may ride on the low swing and even feel bitterness. Not too long after, you once again reach the high swing of the cycle. Same goes for romantic feelings, between a man and woman who love each other deeply even in marriage. Emotions

> **True love is not a feeling that ebbs, it is a commitment to stick with the person, no matter what.**

are feelings and are never stable. In marriage at times, the couple is overflowing in their romantic feelings towards each other and at times the feelings might not be visible however, the real love they have for each other would remain unchanged. True love is not a feeling that ebbs. It is a commitment to stick with the other person no matter what.

If you are attracted to a girl and you smile warmly at her, she will get the message and likely respond. Romantic excitement will build up with the thought of being attractive to the other person. You begin to notice an imbalance in your emotions and before long, you might think, "Why do I feel like this, everything seems right. I must be in love". Mistaking such feelings for real love will be dangerous. It is all about your selfish desires, 'I've never...', 'I must...', 'I think I have...' True love is not selfish, it is not seeking its own desires and it seldom thinks about itself. It is always concerned about the other person's happiness. A major mistake people make when they are infatuated is rushing into a relationship without allowing time to determine whether what they feel is love or infatuation, they might still get away with this unscathed, but they then engage in sex and the damages are done.

Don't Sing It, Show it

Most artists who sing about love songs are definitely not talking about true love. They are referring to the feelings of romantic infatuation. Haven't you figured that out yourself? If only they will make that clarification in their songs, they would be saving a lot of youths from jeopardizing their future. I want to ask you some important questions now, with no disrespect to any one's personality. Have you ever wondered why our TV stars and celebrities jump in and out of relationships dumping one 'girlfriend' or 'boyfriend' for another every now and then? Have you ever heard the family issues of your favourite music and entertainment stars? How are they faring in their marriages? How many of them are divorced already? How many have been labeled with sex scandals? My bonus question; is it that kind of person who wants to teach you about true love in a song?

Many of these so called stars are yet to learn to grow up because they 'fall in' and 'fall out' of relationships as if they were changing clothes. Love as used especially in our environment in recent times is more or less a mirage or fiction. All you get is the fake love- infatuation. Never be deceived by the movies you watch, the music you listen to, the magazines you read and so on. There is more to true love than what is been portrayed by the media and entertainment industry which has taken over our screens. What do you make of an advertorial for a brand of pen that shows a boy and girl getting affectionate? How does a pen help you find true love? It cannot. But it can get you infatuated.

True Love

True love is not a feeling, it is a great commitment. A commitment which is a choice backed up by actions. When you marry, you make a commitment to love your spouse for the remainder of your life. When married couples wake up with no romantic feelings for each other, they do not head straight to the court for a divorce. I will say it again. Love is not a feeling. It requires commitment and with commitment comes romantic feelings.

How to Handle Infatuation

How then do you handle Infatuation? Coming with puberty is the self-appreciation I talked about in Teen Focus #1. A time you begin to fall in love with yourself and think you are attractive to the opposite sex. If you are presently not having any rapport with friends of the opposite sex, be patient, your time would come, sooner or later, but you must be prepared to handle it and deal with it rightly.

When Infatuation sets in, how should you deal with it? When it comes, guard you affections, don't make mistakes. Don't rush into relationships when you are not ready for it. Wait till you are mature enough in every way- physical, emotional, material, financial and spiritual. Wait for the right person, the right circumstance and also for the right time.

The Test of Time

The best way I have proven to effectively handle Infatuation is the test of time. Time tests if your feelings are real or not. I remember my last year of Secondary school when I had a crush on six girls in total, one after another. I was too timid to make my intentions known anyway and thank goodness I didn't. Well it was only a crush anyway. For each of them, I realized that after a while, I lost interest in that person and developed a feeling for another girl. It was then I learnt that letting time pass helps to test the feelings I had. I just let enough time pass and the feelings of infatuation leaves, disappearing into thin air. Feelings of Infatuation do not last for long and it is like a roller coaster ride, while it lasts. It's great but it soon comes to an end. Be sure by the time you come to your senses, you have not made costly mistakes.

When you are no longer sure of your feelings about someone (and even when you think you are), my advice is to withdraw from the person for some time and create some space. There is no specific length of time for which to withdraw. Just give sufficient space to allow you think straight. I do not mean you should completely avoid the person but you should try not to see the person as much as you used to. Reduce your contact points: physical, calls, SMS and chats. Reduce all forms of communication to about 70% and then to about 50% and if possible, much lesser. Do this gradually over a period of time and within that time, keep yourself busy with other things and deliberately focus your thoughts on other things. I am definite about this; the feelings are unlikely to persist if it is infatuation. It would gradually fade away. Real love grows with the passing of time but Infatuation fades.

Real love grows with the passing of time but Infatuation fades.

Dating, What about It?

The natural feeling of wanting to be with someone of the opposite sex brings up the subject of dating. Dating could be said to have different meanings and will depend on the context it is being used and on the culture of the people. It could mean an occasional outing to a social event with a person of the opposite sex who does not always have to be the same person every time and it could also mean having a romantic relationship with a person of the opposite sex. The former is what I will generally refer to as 'going on a date'.

Generally, a date can be defined as a pre-arranged time spent with someone of the opposite sex and there are largely two different kinds.

1. Group Dating: Several boys and girls come together for a specific purpose. They might or might not pair up.

2. Single Dating: A single date is when just one boy goes out with another girl.

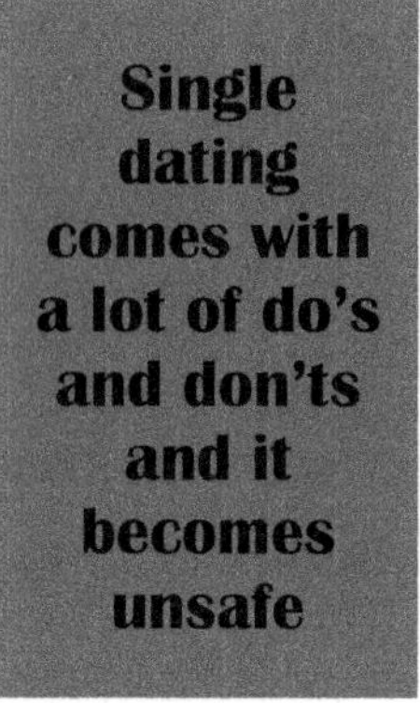

Most times, group dating is always practiced without even taking notice of it. It could be at parties, school functions, picnics, excursions or tours, and even at church. Such avenues are ideal for dating as you get to mix with other people in a secure and safe environment. Dating in the right context has its advantages. George B. Eager in the course, *Love Dating and Marriage*[4] shares a few.

- ♥ It can help you learn to get along socially.
- ♥ It can help you develop a great personality
- ♥ It can help you in choosing a right future partner as you get to know more about others.

I would like to note that as a teenager who is not ready for marriage, group dating would do you more good as you can safely express yourself and yet get all the benefits of dating as stated above without getting into trouble. Single dating comes with a lot of do's and don'ts and it becomes unsafe whereas group dating is good, necessary and needed for your effective participation and integration in the society. There are apparent dangers in single dating and someone might end up marring his or her future happiness by making the wrong choices.

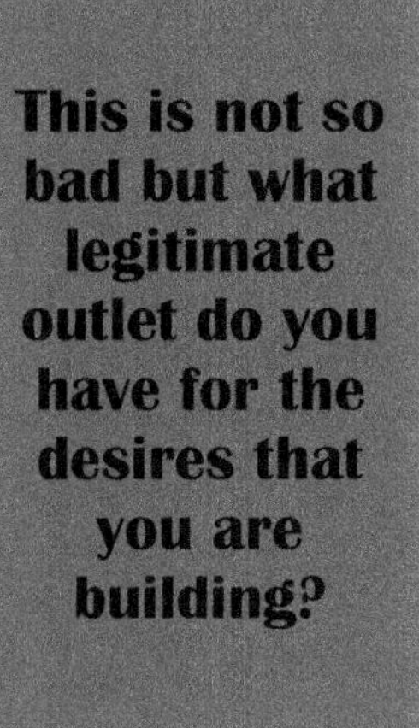

The Dangers of Single Dating

Single Dating makes you spend a lot of time with only one person of the opposite sex (the same person), on the phone, or even through e-mails and letters. As I elaborated earlier on, the attraction would likely grow when you spend a lot of time with the same person of the opposite sex.

"Your dating partner and the things you do becomes a factor that determine the quality of your future life and marriage"- George B. Eager

This is not so bad but what legitimate outlet do you have for the desires that you are building? Are you prepared to take those feelings to their logical conclusion-marriage? Even if you are only friends and nothing more, or maybe intimate friends and you see each other very often and go out on dates, spending lots of time together poses a danger of awakening or arousing feelings of love prematurely. Fanning the flames of desires that cannot be legitimately fulfilled until many years into the future can result in frustration and misery.

> **Fanning the flames of desires that cannot be legitimately fulfilled until many years into the future can result in frustration and misery**

Realizing that you are not ready to commit to someone but you feel like you already have because you are already going out together can be very frustrating. You feel like you are trapped. How do you back out without hurting the other person? Wise King Solomon advises not to awaken love until the time is right.[5]It is sparing you pain and frustration to say that you should not date until you are about old enough to make a marriage commitment.

You Can do without a Date

Yes! You can. Since an unhappy tomorrow and a broken marriage are avoidable, why not do everything necessary to reduce the risks. Single dating when you are not ready for it exposes you to a lot of dangers. There are many factors that can put you under pressure to date especially if most of your peers probably date. The book, *Questions Young people Ask- Answers that work*[6], advises that "a teenager should not begin to date simply because he or she feels pressured to do so". It explains that dating is a serious business and part of the process of selecting a marriage partner. However, marriage could be the last thing on the minds of many young people who are already involved in dating. It also asks a pertinent question. "What good is there in two people of the opposite sex who spend a lot of time together other than to investigate the possibility of marriage?"

But I want to Date?

If you have fully understood all that has been explained in the previous pages and you believe that you are mature enough to date, then there is only one golden rule of thumb. Do not date anyone without your parents' consent. Your parents' oversight will save you a lot of trouble and safeguard you. If it appears your parents will not accept the idea of you dating just yet, then maybe you should hold up a little while longer. Maybe it is not time yet. Remember, there is nothing to rush about getting into a relationship. You are better off waiting and enjoying the company of the opposite sex in group dates and social gatherings.

I've missed it, what do I do?

Based on the new knowledge you have gained, you might need to make some changes and take some drastic steps. Please do. Let your motivation always be the picture of the future you have drawn in Teen focus #3. If you are already dating, or in any kind of relationship with someone and you know or feel you have missed it at some point, it is not too late to retrace your step. You might need to speak to your parents or an adult you can trust to get some advice. You definitely need all the help you can get to get your life back on track.

Sex, What About it?

Sex is God's own idea, God's own plan for child bearing and instituting love between couples. It will be out of place to still believe that sex as a topic should not be discussed with young people. Sadly, there are parents who still believe so. This forces young people to pick up the wrong ideas about sex from their peers and it sets them up for a troubled future.

Sex was not made for a boy and girl, neither was it made for a fiancé and a fiancée but for a man and his wife

Sex was not made for a boy and girl, neither was it made for a fiancé and a fiancée but for a man and his wife. Never engage in pre-marital sex as there are many reasons why you should not. And aside this many reasons, God frowns at it. George B. Eager[7] shares some important reasons. I will share a number of them.

1. Sex before marriage can ruin your chances of knowing Real love: Sex would not help you gain real love; rather real love would delay sex till after marriage. Sex before marriage may ruin your chances of finding real love.

Responsible men would not have sex before marriage and those who do are not likely to marry the girl after they have done it with her. They cannot help thinking how many other persons the girl has been with. The males might not voice this out but this is exactly how they feel.

2. Sex before marriage would keep you from giving the best of you to your spouse: Sex is beyond a physical act. Both parties become one in an intimate experience that make a part of the man forever with the woman and a part of the woman forever with the man. If one engages in sex before marriage, one would then realize that after marriage, you cannot give your marriage mate 100% of yourself. This is because you have given part of yourself to others before marriage. To take

> As a Teen and youth, your purity and not giving in to sex or sexual immorality is your priceless possession

this lightly is ignorance of the fact that we are spiritual beings.

3.   Sex before marriage hurts your self-esteem and gives life-long guilt: As a teen and youth, your purity and not giving in to sex or sexual immorality is your priceless possession. Sometimes, a girl mistakes a boy's sexual desires for the love that she seeks and she gives in, all too often. The boy does not love her nor respect her personality but he just needs someone to satisfy his sexual cravings. If you let yourself to become a victim, you become a 'second hand' or 'used good'. She ends up again with another boy who uses her in her search for love.

"A 42- year old woman wrote. 'When I was young, I fell into sins that have marred my life. My secret sins were committed in my teenage years. I have cried and cried in remorse. If only God would give me peace and take away this awful guilt out of my life."[8]

You may get a few moments of thrilling pleasure out of sex before marriage but it is not worth the price that you would have to pay for it. You are invaluable and should not have a price-tag. Treasure your chastity.

4.   Sex before marriage is hazardous: If you engage in sex before marriage also referred to as pre-marital sex, you are exposed to a higher risk of contracting Human Immune Deficiency Virus (HIV) and other Sexually Transmitted Diseases (STDs). When you sleep with one person, you are actually having sexual contact with everyone your partner has had sex with. If as a boy, you have been with just one girl, the girl could have been with another boy before and the other boy might have been with 6 other girls. Anyone of them could be infected and you can become infected too.

5.   Sex before marriage can result in big problems: There is a great risk of getting pregnant and with this comes the possibility of quitting school and your dreams can all be shattered. You should make up your mind beforehand about not having sex before marriage. No matter what.

6.   Sex before marriage may fool you into marrying the wrong person: Once sex is involved, it clouds your thinking and there is every possibility you do not think well before deciding to marry. Many ladies marry their husbands because he was the one whom she gave her virginity to. In their trying to not have feelings of guilt, they eventually trade their future happiness.

7.   Sex before marriage can ruin your life: This is the sum total of all the consequences of being involved in pre-marital sex. It can ruin your life and shatter your dreams and I know this is the opposite of the future you painted for yourself in Teen Focus #3.

Sex before Marriage is a Sin

It is a sin because it is flouting of God's instructions in the scriptures. This reason is more important than all reasons I have given earlier. And there is nothing anyone says that would change that, not your own opinion, nor mine nor anyone's. In the bible it is called fornication.

> *"Flee fornication. He that commits fornication sins against his own body. Don't you know that your body is the temple of the Holy Spirit who lives in you?"*[9]

> *"Marriage is to be honoured by all. Husband and wives must be faithful to each other. God would judge those who are immoral and those who commit adultery."*[10]

Sexual Immorality

Sex outside marriage and other forms of perversions such as lesbianism, homosexuality, masturbation and the likes are never in God's intended plan for mankind. It is the perversion of mankind and the rejection of God in many instances that make people end up in such a depraved frame of mind. In one of the 2007 editions of the 'Awake!' magazine[11] there is an explicit definition of fornication. "Fornication includes such things as sexual intercourse, oral and anal sex, homosexual acts, masturbation and other acts that clearly involve the misuse of the genitals between two people who are not married to each other"[11]. In this present age a lot of things have changed. Moral standards are falling, but God has not changed and he would not change. Likewise, His standards remain unchanged.[12]

In case you are wondering why you owe God any allegiance and why you cannot live your life the way you want? Why do you have to do what a book- THE BIBLE tells you to? Answers to your questions are in Teen Focus #7. You are not an accident. You are a creation of God and God has an original intention for each creation. You can however exclude yourself from this original plan. It is a choice but you will face the consequences of your actions or inactions.

> **Fornication includes such things as sexual intercourse, oral and anal sex, homosexual acts, masturbation and other acts that clearly involve the misuse of the genitals between two people who are not married to each other**

Avoid Accidents

The best prevention of the consequences of premarital sex is avoidance- 'Abstinence'. Some might hide under the fact that they can continue to have pre-marital sex as long as they are protected with a rubber latex or contraceptive. The truth is condoms are not 100% safe. If you were told that a taxi would have a fatal accident three out of every ten times it is driven with the accidents occurring in no predictable fashion, is it wise to board such a taxi? You can secure your future happiness by avoiding anything that would jeopardize it.

The Sex Drive

As you grow in your teenage years, you reach puberty when you become aware of your sexuality and you become aware of a powerful new force within you, I am referring to the 'Sex Drive'. The sex drive is the appetite for sex that God put within us. It's not dirty or evil. It was God's idea but God only planned that a man would marry a woman so they can share their love together and procreate.

If you are not married- as a teenager, you are probably not, you need to learn to understand and control your sex drive. The sex drive is comparable to the hunger drive, it is not a sin to be hungry but it is a sin to steal food to satisfy your hunger. Satisfying the sex drive-in a wrong way would be a sin against God.

> The sex drive is comparable to the hunger drive. It is not a sin to be hungry but it is a sin to steal food to satisfy your hunger

The Sex –Drive Can Be Controlled

God designed mankind in a way that the sex-drive can be aroused, this should then happen between a husband and wife when they want to, but arousing it outside marriage would likely end up in sin. Stopping from 'going all the way' once the sex drive has been aroused can be frustrating and to go all the way is fornication. Either way, it is no good. You are advised as the bible warns, not to stimulate it outside marriage. And there is also the place of sexual purity which eschews all forms of sexual immorality. Now that you have resolved not engage in the act of sex, it is important to do all that you can to keep yourself sexually pure.

> **The sex drive can be controlled. It can be denied and there are no harmful effects if it is ignored whatsoever.**

The sex drive can be controlled and can be denied. There are no harmful effects if it is ignored whatsoever. It can be denied for an entire lifetime with no ill effects. It is a myth that the sex drive cannot be controlled. I have a couple of close friends who did not have sex until they got married and I have other friends who are in their late twenties and have never engaged in sex. They have not complained about any side-effects, and I am sure they will never have to. Do not let your lack of self-control jeopardize your future.

The sex drive can be stimulated by teasing or caressing each other and touching sensitive parts of each other's bodies. They are various terms that are used to describe this. Such words include 'romance', 'smooching' and 'petting'. When you look at lustful pictures, watch movies, and read magazines designed to produce lust, they build the fires of lust and passion and that fire can burn you without a legitimate way to express it. King Solomon, the wisest man who ever lived on earth asked "Can you carry fire against your chest without burning your clothes? Can you walk on hot coals without burning your feet?"[13] You should be smart enough to know the answers. Desist from every form of sexual activity outside marriage so you can safeguard your future.

The Male drive vs.The Female drive

Men are stimulated and aroused mostly by what they see but ladies are aroused basically by touch. Males can be easily aroused when they see a female dressed in a revealing blouse or short skirt. Some girls do this intentionally. They dress, walk and sit in a way to sexually excite the males. A girl might try to excuse immoral dressing and blame it on the sinful thoughts of the males but it is wrong to act in such provocative ways as it is deliberately causing others to sin.

Unlike men, most ladies are sometimes stimulated largely by what they hear and this makes it easy for men to win them over with their 'sweet talk'. Even when most ladies see the signs that the guy is only playing games with them, he easily convinces her with words and they remain carried away by the lies he has to offer. Many men have mastered this art and know that they can always win over any lady. Something in the woman tells her, 'this guy is lying', but she cannot help it. Their emotions take over. There is an anonymous saying that girls give sex to get love but boys give love to get sex. How true this is but how sad is its consequences. Know that you can never win someone's love by giving in to sex. You only lose a part of yourself and feel cheap.

How To Say No!

Saying 'No' to dating, sex or other perverted sexual acts before marriage is what many young people want to do but quite a few know how to say No!. Not saying 'No' means you get involved but maybe you have no intentions to go far but before you know it, you eventually go all the way. You need to learn to say 'No'. It is a decision you have to make long before you are asked for something you are not prepared to give. It is not only girls that need to say No! Boys also need to say no when they are being lured to do things against their conscience. Tim Waddle in the article *Infatuation or Love*[14] shares these tips to help you learn to effectively say 'No'. To say 'No', it is important to know that fornication is wrong because God says it is.

You also need to be proud of your beliefs. Stand up proudly for what they believe in and make clear statements in words and in actions from the beginning. Keeping your virginity and chastity (if you are no more a virgin) is something to be proud of and you should stand up for it. Never allow anyone to look down on you or joke with you about it, not even someone older.

When you say 'No' is important to note that some boys might misread your refusal as 'playing hard to get'. When boys hear a 'No', they might take it as a challenge, and see you as an obstacle to overcome, so you need to use everything about you; how you dress, how you talk, who you talk to and how you relate with people to say 'No'. Do not be apologetic about it. George B Eager[15] advices that to get the message across to some boys with a wandering hand on your body "may take a slap on the face." It is your life and future happiness that is at stake here. There is no time to look meek or gentle. Be proud of your virginity and keep it. If you have lost it already, then commit to staying sexually pure till marriage.

You can also spare yourself the need to say 'No' at some instances if you have taken some precautions that would make you avoid outright such situations. Separate yourself as much as possible from people who talk about profane things and avoid associations and situations that could be dangerous. Alcohol, dark corners, late nights and the likes are pitfalls. Don't give and entertain some unguarded and incautious looks, words and hugs especially to and from the same set of people. Watch how you dress and do not wear provocative dresses.

Analyze your speech, conduct, associations and the places you frequently visit alone and with your friends. Then ask yourself, "Am I putting myself in a position or unwittingly sending out signals- that would make invitations to engage in sex more likely?" If you think you are, then make moves to make amends and avoid a reoccurrence.

The time to decide to say 'No' is now. You do not have to wait until you get in a difficult situation. Decide to say 'No' now and let this guide your decisions and choices.

There would always be the willpower to stop engaging in pre-marital sex, except you have not decided to. I have once been told this story of a boy who was unable to control his appetite for sex. He was about to engage in the act luring another young lady by saying he loved her and can't control his desires. She however confided in him there and then that she was HIV Positive. You guess what happened. He lost all appetite for sex immediately. Why not exercise that same control initially? It is a fallacy that the sex drive cannot be controlled.

> **Be proud of your virginity and keep it. If you have lost it already, then commit to staying sexually pure till marriage**

WORK TO DO #6

♣ Have you ever been infatuated with persons of the opposite sex and it fizzled out over time? If yes, how many and how long did it last?

♣   What are the things that you can do to protect yourself from situations where you can be asked for sex outside marriage?

ACTIVITY #6

Think about your environment and surroundings and make a list of things that could entice you or make it difficult to want to avoid sex after marriage. Can you discuss this list with your parents or guardian?

TEEN FOCUS #7
GOD & YOU

"Don't let the excitement of youth cause you to forget your creator. Honour him in our youth before you grow old and say, "Life is not pleasant anymore"–Ecc. 12: 1

I am sure you are quick to notice that there is a twist to the title of this Teen Focus different from the others. That is because we as humans and indeed the world exist only because God exists. We are because He is.

You might know so much about God already, but there would always be more to know about Him. You might not know why God should mean anything to you and you might think it is your sole decision to determine how much of your heart you want to give to Him. You might think you do not owe Him any obligation. You should however know that God cares so much about you and loves you with an everlasting love. If you have an objection to that, it is likely because you have not known why and that is pretty fine.

Who or what makes your heart beat? Well, simple answer, If you are good at biology you would know it is the contraction of the cardiac muscles. But what makes these muscles different from every other muscle in the body that makes them undergo involuntary contraction? Some cell variations or specialization. Good answer! So who or what orchestrated this cell differentiation? If you are unsure of the answer, Nature gives its own testimony.

The Testament of Nature; the blue skies, spring time and summer, all creatures- great and small, the large sea whale and the tiny insects, all creeping creatures, the waterfalls and the ocean depths. All things wise and wonderful, the intelligence of man, the diversity of creation and the splendor of natural wonders all point to the existence of an intelligent and supernatural being that exists outside time. The psalmist, King David had this to say about this God.

"Let all that I am praise the Lord. O Lord my God, how great you are! You are robed with honor and majesty; you are dressed in a robe of light. You stretch out the starry curtain of the heavens; you lay out the rafters of your home in the rain clouds. You make the clouds your chariots; you ride upon the wings of the wind. The winds are your messengers; flames of fire are your servants. You placed the world on its foundation so it would never be moved. You clothed the earth with floods of water, water that covered even the mountains. At the sound of your rebuke, the water fled; at the sound of your

thunder, it fled away. Mountains rose and valleys sank to the levels you decreed. Then you set a firm boundary for the seas, so they would never again cover the earth…

You cause grass to grow for the cattle. You cause plants to grow for people to use. You allow them to produce food from the earth, wine to make them glad, and olive oil as lotion for their skin, and bread to give them strength. The trees of the LORD are well cared for… You made the moon to mark the seasons and the sun that knows when to set. You send the darkness, and it becomes night, when all the forest animals prowl about. Then the young lions roar for their food, but they are dependent on God…

O Lord, what a variety of things you have made! In wisdom you have made them all. The earth is full of your creatures. Here is the ocean, vast and wide, teeming with life of every kind, both great and small."[1]

Why Are You Here?

I remember vividly an incident that happened when I was about fourteen years old. I did something my parents thought they should spank me for although I personally did not come to terms with the fact that what I did deserved some spanking. After I got the strokes from my parents who will not tolerate any indiscipline(remember mum is a teacher), I ran into my room and wondered why there was so much suffering in the world (my spanking was on the suffering list) and why there is a heaven and a hell?

I thought of the pain in this world and imagined what pain in hell would look like. I then became scared of ending up in hell. And then I wondered, "Why did God create me? 'Someday I would die and all I would have ever lived for would be gone-vanity'. 'Why didn't God leave me in heaven? Why bring me into this cruel word?' As I continued to ponder and ask my sincere questions, it was as if someone was actually listening to me. Unexplainably, I began to get answers to my questions. An understanding came to me that If God created mankind and made the whole world as beautiful as it is, there must be a reason and a purpose. I wiped the tears from my eyes and made up my mind to find out the reason for my existence. Many years later, I fully understood my purpose for living.

> **Someday I would die and all I would have ever lived for would be gone- Vanity**

Purposeful Living

God gave all men freewill, to make their choices and live as they choose. You may have a great future ahead of you and you may dream to have all you want, wealth, a great home and the best life has to offer. At the end of it all death comes knocking. Is this all Life could be about? The good news is there is more to life. God has a purpose for creating each and every one of us; he has a purpose for you and he has one for me. You might be getting so much out of life already or you might not be satisfied with which cards life has dealt you, you might have a lot of fears and you might be going through troubling times, but know that in the midst of it all, God has good plans for you and never evil plans[2]. His desire is to make you what He has intended before the very creation of the world and he wants to give you the power to overcome sin.

God Made One You

God knows you. He cares for you and knows you by name. You are beautifully and wonderfully made[3]. God made you unique and different from every other person with your own peculiar gifts and talents. He created you and made you to be distinct and unique and there can never be another person exactly like you. God's will for you is for you to enter into fellowship with Him. He loves you and really desires to be your friend if only you would accept His personal invitation to you offered through the sacrifice of Jesus on the cross. If you have not accepted His invitation, make up your mind now. Simply bow your head in prayer, ask God to forgive your sins and give you His Holy Spirit. It is a simple as that.

God's Got Your Back

I heard George Verwer speak at a NIFES (Nigerian Fellowship of Evangelical Students') National Missions conference in 2007. George Verwer is a man passionate about helping people find their purpose on earth and he usually travelled around the world on a ship taking the message of salvation to every continent. He explained that God always has a remedial plan of redemption for all mankind. He did in the Garden of Eden and He still does today. You might think that all hope is lost for you and that you are beyond redemption, but God thinks otherwise. God is able to save to the uttermost and he will give you a clean slate bringing you to a place where your past is forever forgotten. God can give you a fresh start. It is never too late to return to Him. Just get yourself out of the dust of regret and failure and look unto him who is the author and finisher of our faith.[4]He is the God that always takes back prodigal sons and daughters.[5]His mercies are new every morning. He has got your back.

> God can give you a fresh start. It is never too late to return to him

Who could ever Love You Better

By God's decree, you have existence and life. He created you for his own pleasure and purpose. God loves you more than you would ever know. He knows the end from the beginning[6] and really wants the best for you. That is why he has made you as special as you are. No matter how beautiful your dreams are - a good home, an understanding spouse, an established business, great wealth, all-round success, and all you could ever wish for yourself, know that God wants much more for you. You have big dreams; God has bigger dreams for you. He has predestined you to know Him and live in His will so you can live out the bigger dream He has for you.

Some people run from any discourse about God because either they find it hard to give Him priority in their lives or feel this guilt in their hearts. Know that He is a friend you can trust. God does not want to live in heaven but He wants to live in your heart. He wants to be there for you. Some people reach a point in their lives when they have gotten to the end of their ropes. You might be at that point and only hold unto a glimmer of hope that there is a God out there who sees your pain. Be rest assured that God hears you and He will come and save you. God offers you life, hope and a future. You can embrace Him and know a love you would never know outside Him: The fact that God really would come to dwell in your heart for eternity.

You would live forever -as death is only a transition and not the end. Death is a transition to be with the Lord- something far better than the closing remarks of the cartoons and fairy tales- 'happily ever after' with the Lord. One way leads to God, the way of Jesus. Jesus gave up all to give you this opportunity of personally knowing the Lord. Believe Him.

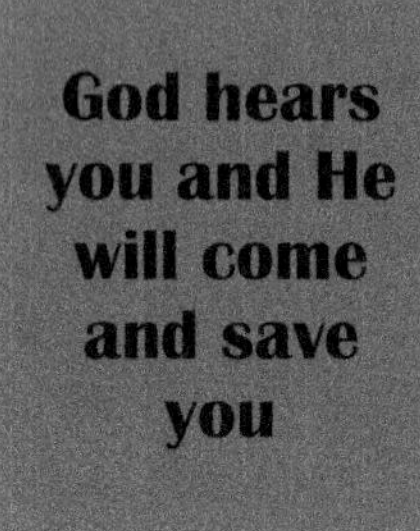

God Speaks

God's word talks extensively about the youth and about childhood. He provides instruction, guidance and direction for life. Let us have a look at some of these words.

- ♣ Don't let the excitement of youth cause you to forget your Creator. Honor him in your youth before you grow old and no longer enjoy living. Ecclesiastes 12: 1
- ♣ A wise youth works hard all summer; a youth who sleeps away the hour of opportunity brings shame. Proverbs 10: 5
- ♣ Let no man despise thy youth; but be thou an example of the believers, in word, in conversation, in charity, in spirit, in faith, in purity. 1 Timothy 4: 12 (KJV)

♣ How can a young person stay pure? By obeying your word and following its rules. Psalm 119: 9

♣ Young people who obey the law are wise; those who seek out worthless companions bring shame to their parents. Proverbs 28: 7

♣ Young man, it's wonderful to be young! Enjoy every minute of it. Do everything you want to do; take it all in. But remember that you must give an account to God for everything you do. So banish grief and pain, but remember that youth with a whole life before him, still faces the threat of meaninglessness. Ecclesiastes. 11: 9-10

♣ Listen, my child, to what your father teaches you. Don't neglect your mother's teaching. What you learn from them will crown you with grace and clothe you with honor. Proverbs. 1:8-9

♣ My child, if sinners entice you, turn your back on them! Proverbs 1:10

♣ Therefore, anyone who becomes as humble as this little child is the greatest in the Kingdom of Heaven.Matthew18:4-5

This page was intentionally left blank.

TEEN CHALLENGES
(HANDLING TOUGH TIMES)

"We are hunted down, but never abandoned by God. We get knocked down, but we are not destroyed" –2 Cor. 4: 9

The Adolescent faces a lot of challenges growing up and a number of them are never able to rise above these challenges as it could grossly affects their future. These challenges come due to societal influences, peers, family and so on. Many kids on the street who appear to have no good support base at home, no hope of attending school, including those who are orphaned, in poverty or homeless are the most vulnerable to these challenges. However, no one is immune of these challenges. The challenges form crossroads at which, depending on the route plied, it either makes or breaks the person. Let us explore some of these challenges that young people could face.

Teen Challenge #1
SEXUAL ABUSE

In 2014, a United Nations report has it that about 120 million girls around the world – slightly more than one in 10, have been raped or sexually assaulted by the age of 20[1].As at 2006, about 73 million boys under the age of 18 experienced "forced sexual intercourse" or other forms of sexual violence. Another report says that in some places, as many as 36% of women and 29% of men had been subjected to some form of sexual victimization during childhood. The majority of the perpetrators were relatives of the victim.

Sexual Abuse is an abuse which forcefully involves people in any form of sexual activity. It is usually against the wishes and rights of the victim and most times the innocence of the victim is taken advantage of. Sexual Abuse includes: Rape and Molestation.

Rape is forcefully luring someone into sex without the consent or consciousness of the victim.

Molestation is fondling or touching the sensitive and private regions of someone without his or her consent.

Abusers- What They Do

Here is a likely way an abuser should likely act. An abuser is likely to be too clever to use force on victims, rather he may prefer to seduce children gradually. He begins by singling out the child for special attention, he may win the trust of the parents, pretend to be interested in the family, soon he grooms the child for abuse right under the nose of the parents by becoming physical with the child i.e. playful wrestling, tickling.

Before long he tells the child to keep little secrets and not to tell anyone about it. He tells him not to tell even his or her parents about it. He warns the child and sometimes scares the child by telling him or her something bad would happen if he tells anyone. When he sees that he has won the trust of the child and that the child is loyal to him, he tries to spend time alone with the child and buys gifts for him or her. Anytime from now, he subtly exploits the child's natural curiosity about sex, plays a 'special' game or exposes the child to pornography.

Teens- What You Should Do

I believe that by now you have understood yourself and the changes at puberty (Teen Focus #1). You should also have understood your relations with your peers and more importantly the opposite sex as discussed this in Teen Focuses #5 and #6. You need to be wise, careful and wary about abusers. Never keep any secrets from your parents. Abusers might even threaten or blackmail you. They might blame you and tell you that it is your fault, that you didn't tell them to stop. They might add, "If you tell your parents, they'll call the police and send me to jail forever" knowing that the child because of ignorance would never wish that for him. They might also say, "It is our secret, if you tell, no one would believe you and if your parents ever do find out, it would hurt them". This is a tactic the Abuser employs knowing that the child would not want anything bad to happen to anybody not even the abuser who is usually a relative. If you keep the secret, it will happen again and again until you become used to it and come to accept it as normal. The child no longer resists and is compensated by the Abuser with more gifts. This can go on for years without anyone finding out. There are many adults who now regret their childhood because they have been molested, abused or raped. You can change that. Do not keep any of such secrets. Tell an adult you can trust about it if for any reason you cannot tell your parents. Sometimes, it is either of the father or mother that abuses their own child.

My dear teen, the first step to overcoming this abuse is to tell someone, especially your parents. The Abuser would never stop as long as you don't tell anybody and he could later begin to threaten you. If you don't tell someone, you would lose your self-esteem and you would regret this so much later in life. Secure your future happiness by telling someone older than you who can help you out.

Secure your future happiness by telling someone older than you who can help you out

Never let anyone touch you in a way that's wrong or makes you feel uncomfortable. The parts of your body that a bathing suit covers are private and special, not toys, they are not funny and they are nothing to be shameful about. Abusers might also tell you to touch them in ways that are wrong. Don't give in and immediately report he incidence to someone you think you can trust and that would listen to you. If it is one of your parents that abuse you, ensure you tell the other person or try to tell another adult who can find help for you.

Parents and Guardians

As a parent or guardian, you need to ensure you keep close watch over your children. Having said that be careful of being too suspicious of people to an extent where you begin to raise false alarms. Wisdom is required in this regard. You must however ensure you know everything happening to your child and always talk to him or her to ensure that he has no secrets he would not let you hear about. Watch over your child especially if there other persons who take custody of him when you go to work or on trips. Abusers can be males or females, most times relatives and sometimes strangers. Relatives have an easier access to your children and can earn their trust and yours. They can pick on children as young as a few months old usually starting with molesting the child. Be careful about who you put your children in their care, and who you allow your kids to spend holidays with.

Keep a protective eye over your children, teach them and educate them on these issues before hand as much as they can understand depending on their age. Do not hold back from teaching your child about sex as soon as you see your child or ward begins to ask questions. Praise Fowowe, a sex education expert advices that parents should teach sex education from age one till the late teens using various approaches and languages that the child would understand. He advises that long before your children enter their teens, between 8 and 12 years old. He writes in one of his sexual abuse education series "...you teach your children about good touch, bad touch and confusing touch. Instruct them to avoid full hug or sitting on anyone's laps. They must resist it when someone tries to tickle them and tell your girl child that the reward for anyone trying to touch her breast is a dirty slap". Many parents have pushed the children into the hands of 'predators 'by not educating them beforehand and answering their questions. Do not be a victim.

Teen Challenge#2

MASTURBATION

Churchill Livingstone describes masturbation as self-production of "sexual excitement or friction of the genitals". It is an act of exciting the genital organs through unnatural means. It is to produce self-abuse. It is leading one's self to sexual excitement by creating fantasies through illicit imaginations, replaying a memory of sexual act, a lover or admirer, a story of sex in books, magazines or other sexual situations. It is common to both sexes

Have you found yourself fondling with your genitals using your hands or any material while running wild in your imaginations about sex, or imagining yourself with someone in a sexual act? Then you have been masturbating.

It is generally believed to be a normal occurrence in adolescence but the truth is it becomes more of an addiction and as I would put it all negative addictions makes one no longer in control of oneself and is in a sort of bondage. The imagination attached with it also clouds the memory and affects one's thinking and it becomes much more difficult to resist pre-marital sex. The society we are in tries to lower moral standards and say there is nothing wrong with masturbation but the truth would always remain the truth. There is nothing right about shameful acts that we cannot proudly say in the open. Others, especially females use sex toys to stimulate themselves and this also falls in this category of masturbation: self-stimulation to derive sexual pleasure.

Masturbation is an act that comes with a feeling of shame and guilt. Many young people male and female have struggled with masturbation and have been able to overcome it with God's help and counseling. You can too. Masturbation has emotional dis-benefits and can affect your sex life when you become married.

What To Do

Don't let the guilt burden your heart so much that you can't get out of it any longer. Take to heart especially if you are already trying to stop it but it looks like you can't help it. Do not give up courage and don't give up the fight.

Shame might make it difficult for you to bring up the subject even with a confidant. If you do not discuss it with someone, the feeling of guilt might plague you for many years and seriously affect your relationships with others." Tell someone mature about it preferably your parents. Avoid looking at things that stimulate improper desires. Engage your mind to think of other more important and productive matters.

It is important for parents to note that proper and adequate sex education during pre-teen and teen years prepares your child well ahead to handle this tough challenge of the youth.

Teen Challenge #3

DRUG, ALCOHOL& TOBACCO ADDICTION

It's everywhere around us, daily we see people struggling with drug, and alcohol addiction. Drugs, alcohol and cigarettes are a threat to human life. It may seem like the cool thing to do but that kind of 'cool' has a price tag. Drugs and alcohol can cause brain damage and it is known that smoking eventually leads to cancer of the lungs and many other diseases. Drugs, alcohol and tobacco are all addictive. They take hold of your life until you can't say 'No' anymore.

The Process

It starts so simply, just one cigarette, maybe a little weed, and a sniff of glut or downing a drink in a dare. Just one shot anyway. But now it goes too far. You take too much every day and you know it. You need it more and more. You are out of control and you don't know what to do.

It's like that with addiction to drugs, alcohol and cigarette. They sneak up unto you until you are powerless.

Parents and Guardians

How do you help yourself as a teenager or young person and how do you as a parent help your teenager who is facing this challenge.

♥ **Help rather than Punish:** Seek ways to help the young person overcome addiction. Punishing him should not be an issue to consider as it would only make matters worse.

- ♥ **Therapy:** Finding the right therapy is critical- the counseling needs to be supportive as well as parents and siblings. A counselor or doctor with training might do or there might be need for the combination of different therapy methods. A good therapist or counselor would work towards finding the cause of the addiction.

- ♥ **Build Self- Esteem:** Reinforce your teen's strengths and find ways to make them laugh. Encourage participation in volunteer projects and social activities.

- ♥ **Ensure effective communication:** Listen to your child and other than overreacting to what they share and as a good parent be cognizant of what they share as to whether they need support, comfort, new ideas, or just someone to listen to them. Provide opportunities for communication that is neutral and less intense such as when taking a walk or participating in an activity together.

- ♥ **Tighter Parenting:** Whatever the underlying cause for your teen's addiction problems, tighter parenting needs to be implemented so as not to enable them to continue their poor choices. If you do not have house rules relating to chores, homework, driving and school, create one. If you have, go over them and check to see if they probably need to be made more explicit with details such as who, what and when.

- ♥ **Let go off blame:** Parents can become immobilized through issues of self-blame. During recovery, your child needs you to be strong and supportive, you should not dwell on the things you had not done in the past that led to the present situation but you should dwell on the things you should start doing to help.

- ♥ **Parent support and self-care:** Parenting any child is difficult and parenting a teen with drug addictions or chemical dependencies can be overwhelming. Parents become emotionally drained and need to find ways to replenish themselves. Find time to spend time with your spouse, take a walk, and take time to relax. A strong and focused parent. Take time to speak with other parents who could offer valuable advice and encouragement or enroll with a counselor who would help you make the work easier.

Parenting your teen through the challenges of addiction would be intensely difficult for you, your teen and the rest of the family- but with dedication and firmness you would be surrounding them with the elements they need to help them fight their addiction.

Teen Challenge #4
LOW SELF – ESTEEM

'I am ugly.' 'I am no good at sports or in my schoolwork'. 'I am not good at anything'. 'I am fat'. Have you ever said these words to yourself? Perhaps you have looked yourself in the mirror and wished you were someone else. Maybe you wished you were a famous actor or sports hero and felt you were not good enough for anything. Many people have once wished that they could change at least one physical feature, their nose, their complexion, height, weight or one other thing. I used to dislike my face ridden with pimples and acne. I always wished I did not have to battle with that.

Self-esteem is a product of perception: how you see yourself. You might have a physical challenge that others probably do not care about maybe you've got a big nose, or head. Or it could be that you have a habit that seems unpleasant. You might begin to look down on yourself when you think others do not appreciate you. You begin to have a wrong perception about yourself.

The opposite which is a high self-esteem is having confidence in yourself accepting your strengths and weakness alike while a low Self Esteem is the opposite: looking down on yourself and not being able to come to terms with your weaknesses. A good high Self Esteem is needed for a vibrant life.

Improving Your Self Image

1.Be patient with yourself

2.Set goals that can be accomplished and successful

3.Reward your successes

4.Meet and establish new friends

5.Use your family as your support system. They always accept you, so learn to see yourself as someone with high self-esteem amidst your family members

6.Make a decision to change what you do not like about yourself.

7.Realize that there is no other person like you. God made us all unique in different ways with different gifts.

This page was intentionally left blank.

NOTES

TEEN FOCUS #1: You & Yourself

1. S. D Olaitan, C. O Mbaly, *Junior Secondary Home Economics*. West African Book Publishers, 2001
2. Dorothy Law Nolte, (1972/1975).*Children learn What They Live*. Author approved short version.

TEEN FOCUS #2: You & Your Home

1. Praise George, *Rules for Teens*. Success World Limited

TEEN FOCUS #3: You & Your Future

1. ZigZiglar, (1975). *SeeYou at the Top*.Pelican Publishing
2. *Ibid* 1.
3. Luke 12:15, (GNB); Paraphrased
4. Galatians 6: 7 (GNB); Paraphrased
5. Brian Tracy, (1997). *Eat that Frog*. Berrett-Koehler Publishers

TEEN FOCUS #4: You & Your Education

1. ZigZiglar, (2001). *You Can Reach the Top*. Riveroak Publishing
2. Ben Carson, (1990). *Gifted Hands: The Ben Carson Story*, Review and Herald Publishing Association.
3. Ben Carson, (1996). *Think Big*, Zondervan Publishing.
4. KehindeOdeniyi, (2007). *The Insider's Guide to University Success*. Success World Limited.

5. 1 Corinthian 15:33

TEEN FOCUS #5: You & Your Friends

1. *Book of Hope*, Book of Hope International.www.hopenet.com
2. Genesis 2: 18 (GNB); Paraphrased
3. Vertical Thought, (Oct. 2006). *The Friendship Formula*.United Church of God.
4. *QuestionsYoung People Ask- Answers that Work*, (2008) Watchtower Bible & Tract Society.Volume 1.
5. Proverbs 1: 10

TEEN FOCUS #6: You &The Opposite Sex

1. Genesis 2:26-28.
2. Awake, (Mar. 2007). *Youth*.Watchtower Bible & Tract Society.
3. Ann Landers, (Oct 3, 1968). *Dear Ann*. Atlanta Journal.
4. George B. Eager, (1987)*Love, Dating and Marriage*.The Mailbox Club Inc.
5. Songs of Solomon 8: 4
6. *QuestionsYoung People Ask- Answers that Work*, (2008) Watchtower Bible & Tract Society.Volume 1.
7. *Ibid* 4.
8. Ann Landers, (1963). *Ann Landers talks to Teenagers about Sex*, Prentice-Hal, Inc.
9. 1 Corinthian 6: 18
10. Hebrew 13: 4
11. *Ibid* 2.

12. Numbers 23: 19; Paraphrased
13. Proverbs 6: 27-28 (GNB)
14. Tim Waddle, (Dec. 2006). *Infatuation or Love*, Vertical Thought.United Church of God.
15. *Ibid* 4.

TEEN FOCUS #7:God & You
1. Psalm 104: 1-25
2. Jeremiah 29: 11; Paraphrased
3. Psalm 139: 6 (KJV); Paraphrased
4. Hebrew 12: 2 (KJV)
5. Luke 15: 11-32
6. Isaiah 46: 10

TEEN FOCUS #8:Teen Challenges
- BBC News, www.bbc.com/news/world-29071073
- Chris T. Orodiji, *Sex, Rape & Masturbation*. Armstrong Plus communication
- Vertical Thought, (Oct. 2006). *The Friendship Formula*.United Church of God.
- *QuestionsYoung People Ask- Answers that Work*, (2008) Watchtower Bible & Tract Society. Volume 1.
- "Peer Educators Training Manual," Goods supply.
- *Reports on the global HIV/AIDS epidemic 2000.*
- Praise Fowowe, Centre for Sex Education and Family Life. www.mindandmouth.com

JOIN THECONVERSATION

Get access to information
and updates about the book

+

Drop your comments and
ask questions

+

Join the community of
other young teenagers and
adults

**For Teenagers, young persons and adults who care
about them**

WEBSITE: www.purposefulteen.wordpress.com
TWITTER: @Purposeful_Teen
FACEBOOK: Purposeful Teen
EMAIL: Purposefulteen@gmail.com

Ebenezer communicates with passion and apt. He deeply connects with his audience, inspires and motivates to stir up action. He believes true motivation and inspiration would make the audience take the bold steps required to achieve results, pursue their dreams and reach their goals. Ebenezer is open to invitations to speak to your youth audience; trainings, workshops, conferences, youth camps, in schools and so on.

PASSION AREAS

Purpose Discovery | Academic Excellence | Mentoring
Relationships, Dating, and Sex Issues | Entrepreneurship
Career Counseling |Leadership & Capacity building

For enquiries & bookings contact:

5, Nureni Aka Street, I.L.O
Sango Ota, Ogun State, Nigeria
ebennyinc@yahoo.com | P.O.Box 125, Ota
+2348070002309 | +2348038555960